Up to Me

Other books by this Author:

Perfect Choice

Up to Me

A unique approach to self-development that aims to renew confidence, improve relationships and provide profound insights into how to achieve your full potential.

Mary Ancillette

Life-Changing Moment

Completely Novel

Up to Me

First published in Great Britain in 2013 by

Completely Novel

ISBN 978-1-849-144223

All names and many of the circumstances are changed for the privacy of the clients.

This book is dedicated to the people I most adore - may they prosper in the richness of happiness.

Content

With Thanks

. . . .

Often we come to this part in a book and gloss over it, uninterested in the importance of acknowledgment. But the more we become attuned to our sense of purpose, the more we appreciate the significance of thanks.

My journey started some while back, even before I first realised it, and as a result I couldn't begin to imagine how many people have contributed to my development and hence the Life-Changing Moment concept. But in terms of 'Up To Me' there have been several people who have not only given of themselves unselfishly but had a direct and positive influence.

My heartfelt thanks go to Lizzy and to Bryan for their friendship and input. Without them this book may never have been written. They have undoubtedly been seminal in my development and career and I shall always be grateful.

John, my father, has been loyally supportive, spending many an hour mulling over ideas with me, encouraging me to the next level with no thought for himself. I am eternally grateful.

As for my children, Alex, Imogen and Mike, their love and belief in me not only fuel my desire to help others but encourage me to improve on myself. They have, independently of one another, contributed to this book in ways even they are not aware of, and I love them so much.

Sheila, my dear friend and copy-editor, has worked tirelessly, often into the night, to improve on my literacy … what would I have done without her?

And Esther Clark-van Oostrum for her uplifting drawings, I thank you so much.

But my most gracious thanks goes to all the people who have made my learning applicable, whether through my own experiences or working with my clients. I can't thank you enough. You have fulfilled my purpose.

www.maryancillette.com

Introduction

The purpose of this book is not only to introduce the wisdom that surrounds us all, but to encourage and empower excellence.

To excel is a powerful form of self where self-belief and confidence exceed normal bounds and spread into fields of love, joy, energy and freedom. We're all healers of a sort and as such are extraordinary people. But we often 'forget' this in the race to been seen as successful, challenging ourselves with nonsensical arguments just to be proved correct when all the while it's the *experience* that counts.

Growth in any format is wonderful and primarily what this book is about. If we don't respect ourselves enough by acknowledging this then we might as well give up.

By committing to resolve the dichotomy within us we're not only abiding by the rules of the 'old ways,' admiring strength of character and love in the process, but authenticating true sense of self. We're taking responsibility for who we are and making honesty the decision maker, thereby ensuring our success.

Continuity of character and a steadfast approach brings the greatest results. By grasping every opportunity we're making this world a better place.

Within the text is hidden a wealth of information for our use. Don't assume it'll be obvious for the sceptics among us, but hopefully in time they'll come to see the true value of its worth. We're going to approach this compassionately, teasing out the strands to work on much like freeing a log jam in a river. We don't have to shift every log, just the few that cause the blockage.

We'll discover sides to us that have long since been forgotten and learn to incorporate them back into our life. Some may feel challenged by this, fearful of the consequences, but there really is nothing to fear, this is a purely natural response to spiritual development. There's no need for comparisons or one-upmanship, we're all developing people and as such will reach our potential soon enough. But should there be any sense of discomfort, pull back on the learning for a while and allow the excellence already achieved to consolidate. It won't be long before you're ready to pick up the gauntlet again!

We're here to expand human consciousness and thus need to commune openly with our higher selves. We're going to work alongside the greatest teachers who are quite literally waiting to assist. If you're not comfortable with this, ask yourself, does lack of confidence and/or self-belief come into it? I'm not challenging anyone's spiritual or religious beliefs at this stage, just highlighting the possibility that we're all communing on higher realms and need to respect this. By working on ourselves in this way we're being openly honest and respectful of all those we care about and come in contact with, without imprinting negatively on anyone. It's a perfect example of human awareness and I'm proud to be a part of it.

We need to decide our own route and the speed we wish to travel. More often than not we're swept along with the crowd but from now we're going to live more *purposefully* where strength of resolve far outstrips other people's expectations of us. We're going to live more modestly, where traditions and values are respected alongside will, encouraging a new and exemplified state of self. We're extraordinary people, so why not acknowledge it?

To reach this wonderful state of self-empowerment we need to relinquish the desire to be spoon-fed and appreciate that growth stems from self. We're not turning to others to assist, that would be self-defeating, but aim to regain knowledge of self so *we* can make the right choice. This book is structured compassionately to provide the best way to accomplish this without compromising self or others. It's a suggestion rather than a must, so use it as you wish.

We don't have to experience every little bump in the road to gain the wisdom from the route. In time we'll learn to navigate it so expertly as to become a teacher in our own right. The journey may seem quite arduous at times, so be prepared for this; we're aiming for a reliable route where true depth of meaning is discovered through honesty and hard work, thereby ensuring greater results.

Don't think you're alone with this. We're all developing and as such are working simultaneously on subliminal levels to encourage communion of spirit in line with our new resolution for growth. We're not trying to lead but are attempting to be seen as examples to learn from.

I'm not advocating solidarity to the extent that expansion of self becomes our sole purpose but to be subjective enough so that all can benefit. By understanding the extremities of traits and how to lessen their hold on us we're developing into far kinder people without having to concern ourselves with conformity and choice for us; we're individual and as such are unique. If I can help find just some of the answers without dictating the route then I've achieved what I set out to.

Empowerment may not seem instantly attainable or, dare I say, of importance, but as we progress we'll come to see its true worth: developing and witnessing first-hand how powerful and appealing it is to purify one's intentions and balance one's own character traits. I'm not proposing sweeping changes but a steadfast approach that is easy to maintain. After all, we wouldn't want to add to the already frenetic pace of this world by misunderstanding what we're doing!

This book is about appreciating ourselves and our full potentials without imprinting negatively on anyone else.

It's a huge task and one we can accomplish if we *want* to, but it takes effort and the need to be honest. If we're not prepared to look innermost for the answers it's unlikely we'll achieve this state of wonderment purely because we're hooked on apportioning blame, looking at others as our nemesis rather than taking responsibility for ourselves.

And that's the true nub of this, response-ability; a play on words that's as mocking as it is funny, since we each have the potential to make the best of ourselves so long as we're 'responsible' for our makeup and accept we have the 'ability' to change it.

True invocation may not be the most pertinent expression to use at this point but with perseverance and grace we'll come to appreciate how dynamic it is, enveloping us with a sense of change and trust that encourages confidence and self-worth.

In order to achieve this we need to ensure balance. It's a common enough expression but do we understand its pre-eminence in terms of success? It implies change but not in the sense of loss; it encapsulates our true sense of self and lays out a template for us to follow.

To understand the concept of balance is the kingpin of spiritual development and, no matter where we focus, balance will always have its place. But we're not going to examine balance alone, as there are many other factors that need to be incorporated into our approach to provide a much firmer base.

Duality is just one aspect, as it's with these opposing forces that we can make a difference. Positive-negative and masculine-feminine are just two of many examples we can use to better our prospects and make us unique. If we accept that developing life lies within a symbiotic balance of duality, then we're on the path to enlightenment.

To help, we'll use a simple image of a playground seesaw: it's not perfect, but provides a good enough model from which to progress. In time we'll adapt to a more comprehensive approach - but that's for another book.

The book is broken down into sections, and has exercises throughout. Take the opportunity to work through the whole book at your own pace before dipping back and forth. Work individually or as a group, but, should you wish further support, there will be plenty of information available through the website.

Life takes on a different meaning once we acknowledge the effects of spiritual investment and this book is just the start of it.

This is a life-changing moment! Take from it what you will and may I wish you every success.

www.maryancillette.com

SECTION ONE

Section One

Chapter 1 - Introduction to balance

What does being in balance mean to you?

In this first section I'm going to show you an effective way to bring yourself into balance without any emotional upset or self-judgement. I'm not proposing that this is the only way to achieve this, but it's a unique approach that's been used successfully by many of my clients. It's easy to follow and can be used on many levels, once you've understood the principles, either on your own or with a therapist. As long as you're prepared to be honest with yourself you can't fail to benefit.

To begin with we should consider the question at the start of this chapter. Everyone has a different viewpoint on what being in balance truly means, so let this be a time to reflect on what it means to you.

As I mentioned in the introduction, it's a good idea to work through the whole book before going back and re-reading any chapters that are more pertinent to you. This not only ensures that you have a good understanding of the whole framework of the process, but provides further progressive insights into your self-development.

Try to complete each exercise as it comes along. Being proactive in the exercises will help your transition into balance – your point of oneness – more swiftly. I'm sure it comes as no surprise to hear that we learn best when we're involved in a task rather than being a mere bystander. So with this in mind I'd like you to consider this question and write your thoughts in the box.

What does being in balance mean to me?

Understanding what we're trying to achieve gives us a focus, a target to aim at, so that we get the most out of our studies. Now that we have a defined purpose we'll continue.

Character traits are inherent within all of us. Some are considered endearing, others less so, but it's not how acceptable each characteristic is that concerns us, so much as how strongly they appear and what we're prepared to do about them.

We all have aspects of ourselves that are out of kilter. However, in order to balance our traits, we need to appreciate the weight of each of them and look at how they present in us so that we can with compassion and understanding bring them back towards the middle, our place of comfort. This may on the surface appear a simple concept, as all high level concepts often do, but it'll require a degree of dedication and complete honesty to implement. Denying that we have certain characteristics, or trying to *control* them as a way to dampen their obviousness isn't the answer. It may subdue them in the short term under the false premise that we aren't influenced by them, but it doesn't convince anyone, least of all our inner self, which automatically senses any dishonesty.

We need to create a solid base to work from. Much like building a house that's able to weather all storms, our foundations need to be firm. So to start this, our non-judgemental look at how our characteristics appear will be a life-changing moment.

Characteristics that have long been thought of as unpleasant or tragic can actually turn out to be some of our best character traits once they've been brought into balance. This alone shows us how beneficial self-development is. None of us likes to feel disgruntled or out of sorts, but sadly that's just what happens if we neglect our spiritual self. By attaining a far more 'rounded approach,' we'll gain greater confidence, trust and belief in who we are, without conflicting with our life-purpose or identity. Joy, peace and a place of comfort are redeeming elements in this fast-paced world of stress and dramas!

Self-development is not about self-focus to the exclusion of others; it's about balancing our traits and behaviours that would otherwise go undetected if we didn't have interaction with friends, family, work colleagues or even strangers to bring them to the surface. I'm sure there have been times in your life when a person has 'pushed your buttons', where you've felt less than happy with your own response, where you've felt that the other person was *responsible* for your out-of-character outburst rather than accepting responsibility for it yourself.

It's at times like these that we need to observe our behaviours as they are wonderful moments of clarity where we can gather so much information for our self-development. If we really want to progress and improve our own prospects, then it's at this level that we need to start to work.

"The key to keeping your balance is knowing when you have lost it"
Anonymous

It's always so much easier to see 'fault' in someone else than to recognise it in ourselves. But this isn't about anyone else: it's about seeing the truth in our own given characteristics and coming to the realisation of how beautiful and beneficial spiritual motivation really is. None of this is about blaming someone else; all of it is about recognising oneself. If we consider at any point that we have switched our attention, then we need to bring ourselves back into focus.

We gain invaluable information when monitoring our emotional response to other people's character traits. So from this perspective we do need to be observant of traits in other people, *but not from the point of passing judgement*. If we sense a strong emotional response within ourselves when witnessing someone else's traits, it's confirmation that there is an aspect of that same characteristic held within us that needs to be brought into balance. Don't worry at this point about how it's been exposed, as each characteristic will present itself differently from person to person, just be aware it indicates an aspect in you. There are always exceptions to every rule, so don't take this too literally, but as a general guideline it's very helpful.

A technique that you might find very useful when starting out is detachment. Being too close to a subject not only reduces our perspective but lends itself to self-criticism, which is unhelpful. Imagine that you're watching yourself on a television screen for example, this may help you attain the level of honesty that's required to gain the most from your development. Honesty is enormously important through all of this, as is sensitivity and self-respect.

Initially we'll use the image of a seesaw. As I explained in the introduction, it's not an ideal representation of what we're trying to achieve, and as we progress we'll need to use a more complex paradigm, but it's a good working model to get us started.

The point of balance that we wish for is in the middle, at the fulcrum. Imagine you're standing on a seesaw with one foot either side of the fulcrum. As you rock from one leg to the other the seesaw moves, lowering the extremities of it nearer the ground, first on one side and then the other. Although the range of movement at the far ends of the seesaw is quite apparent, the little movement at the fulcrum is almost imperceptible. This is an important point and one we'll come back to regularly as by lessening the influence of a given characteristic, and its antonym (its opposite characteristic), we're effectively moving the weight of them inwards towards the fulcrum of our seesaw.

Not only will this have the glorious effect of lessening the extremes of our behaviour but we'll feel generally more peaceful – in other words, it eases some of the burden of being so much out of balance. And, perhaps even more astoundingly, the obvious swing that is witnessed by others as we go first from one end of the seesaw to the other becomes less noticeable as we move the characteristic towards the fulcrum, bringing about balance.

With every trait there is its opposite – its antonym. And it's with these two characteristics that we can start to evaluate our true state. This isn't going to be easy for some, as to acknowledge even from a distance their less favourable aspects can be quite difficult. But there's no need for fear of judgement, you're incredibly brave to undertake such a comprehensive form of self-development and no one is going to make fun of you. More to the point, this is your self-progression, done at your pace and no one needs to know you're even doing it if you don't want them to. But when they see the transformational process start to unfold, they'll be intrigued as to how you're achieving this!

So don't be nervous, there's nothing to get wrong and there's no place for self-judgement or self-reprimand. Of course it will seem awkward at times to admit to yourself that you have these characteristics - we all feel this at some point, but as we said before, it's blinkers off, time to be honest and, above all, respectful to yourself.

(There is a way that we can do this if you're less able to be honest with yourself, but let's try this way for now, and see how we go.)

So once we've a chosen characteristic for one side, and the antonym for the other, where do we place them on our image of a seesaw? If we feel that either of the characteristics holds much weight, then we'd be inclined to place it away from the middle. Likewise if it has little influence it would be nearer.

Let us use an example:

Marjorie finds it hard to speak up about what she wants from a friendship, often feeling pushed to go to parties that aren't her type of thing. Her friend, Sophie, wants her to go so that she has a companion to party with. When asked how she feels about herself when thinking about this, Marjorie instantly says weak.

So weak is the characteristic we will work with, and when asked the antonym, she says strong.

So our seesaw will look like this

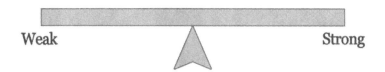

Now that we've established the basic model we need to know where to place the weight of each characteristic. This represents how much influence each characteristic has on Marjorie, and provides a point to work from.

In order to do this, we need to consider the moments when the trait is most obvious, has the greatest influence, and find a place for it to rest on our seesaw. So, for Marjorie, it's the time when she felt 'weak' for not speaking up. Remember that our goal is to get towards the middle, so the further out she places herself, the more it will reflect on her inability to be balanced.

Her first response when shown this schematic was to place herself three quarters of the way along towards the outmost position, showing that the influence this characteristic has upon her is fairly weighty.

Remember there's no sense of self-judgement going on here, just an honest appraisal of self. When working on this, try to listen to your gut instinct first, as it's usually correct. Yes, we can negotiate with ourselves up or down afterwards, but all of my experience indicates that we tend to know instinctively and immediately where to place each trait.

Once we've got this marked on the seesaw we need to examine its antonym. She used the word 'strong' so we'll look at times when she felt this. When asked for an example she said, 'When my mother asks to meet me for a coffee or lunch.' Marjorie went on to explain that she turns her down continuously, claiming she is too tired or busy. She admitted that she is uninterested in her mother's feelings.

Before we go any further I need to explain that an individual's perception is all that matters when it comes to self-development. It's not for us, as outsiders reading this, to decipher other aspects on her behalf, or to pass judgement on whether we agree with their interpretation. Some may use the word strong or weak in totally different contexts, and as we go further we'll strip this down even more so there's a list of words or phrases to help quantify the positions Marjorie has placed herself in. But for now we will keep it simple.

Now that Marjorie has decided on a moment when she felt her 'strong' tendency is apparent, she was ready to place the weight of it on the other side of the seesaw, again using her intuition as guidance.

Now her seesaw looks like this:

From this it's instantly obvious that, although Marjorie has the ability to speak up sometimes, with certain people or circumstances she is prone to subservience. This swing from one extreme to the other will create much discomfort within her and give her a sense of being one-sided, whilst those around her may consider she is inconsistent.

This is a very simplistic image of her position, for of course there are many other factors that need to be considered before she'll be able to bring her characteristic towards the middle. But this is the start of her work using the seesaw. In the following chapter we'll progress with this further.

One thing for certain is the fact that she has identified this characteristic, and the cohesive factor, and is thus already in the process of bringing these traits into balance.

There's no wrong or right way to work with this book. If you're happy to get to the crux of a characteristic then that's fantastic, if you'd prefer to tinker around the edges for a while, working through the layers like peeling away an onion, then that's fine also. Do what feels comfortable and allow your intuition, which is inherent within each of us, to guide you.

I'll give you another example:

John was used to getting his own way, but became upset when someone accused him of being selfish. Rather than accept the other person's viewpoint, he got upset and started to shout back obscenities as a way to deflect attention from his own inadequacies (his own sense of imbalance).

From this we can extract various character traits, but for this purpose we'll take one - argumentative.

Now we need to find its antonym, its opposite influence, let's say placid.

So his seesaw would look like this:

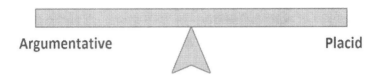

Argumentative   Placid

Exercise

In this exercise, you'll be using some recent incidents in your life to uncover some character traits. Think about times where you've felt less than happy about a situation. You won't have to delve too far to see that many characteristics are displayed continuously throughout our lifetime. Addressing some of the more poignant ones and lessening their weights will be a life-changing experience.

If you feel that you may not be ready to plunge straight in with the 'big ones' just yet, why not consider a few less influential traits and start with them? Or, if you prefer, go to the back of the book where some of the more common traits and characteristics are listed together with their antonyms.

Take an experience when you've felt uncomfortable, one that created an unpleasant emotional response within you (remembering that this is your inherent early warning system talking to you, trying to get you to take heed). From that experience, work out your main character trait from your behaviour, and then look to its antonym. Don't worry about finding a time when you displayed the antonym in your behaviour - at this stage, all we're doing is recognising the aspects. Now label your seesaw with the characteristics at either end.

Do this with several other incidents to uncover various traits and antonyms, and place them on individual seesaws, ready to start working on them.

Dwell on this

One of the most beautiful effects of self-development is the realisation that we don't need to prove anything to anyone: we are who we are, and, as such, are perfect.

Section One

Chapter 2 – Harmful thoughts

In this chapter we're going to continue balancing our traits using the seesaw. Balance is all around us - whether it's nature, maths, science or nutrition, there's no getting away from its influence. But how often do we consider its effect on our long-term health and general sense of well-being?

Whether we're building a castle or playing an instrument, it's the end result that needs to be considered. There'd be little point to a moat that's half-finished, or a stringed instrument without its strings. So why choose to stay incomplete if there's a wonderful way to address this?

Sadly, most of us are prepared to settle for less than our full potential under the guise that we're too old and set in our ways, or can't be held responsible, or we simply don't have the courage or enough self-belief to see the dream in the first place. Being released from these constraints is a glorious moment where expectations - whether set by us, our friends or society - and self-limiting behaviours are pushed aside in freeing our true potential: truly a life-changing moment!

As developing people we need to lead without dictating, to contain without confining and to affirm without contradiction. With positivity and compassion we can resolve the character traits that have caused us so many problems in the past and free ourselves from the negative behaviour associated with them. Not only will this improve our levels of confidence and self-esteem, but our health and sense of well-being will flourish as a result.

We're leading lights in the search for freedom and as such have a responsibility to fulfil. Whether we wish to help people on a daily basis or simply set an example, every step we take towards balance provides a lasting, positive effect on all those we come into contact with. Much like throwing a pebble into a still pond, the ripples reach out far and wide to the most unexpected people and can help improve their sense of self too.

So in order to progress, we need to know how to separate the thoughts in our heads from the characteristics themselves to help bring them into balance. We also need to appreciate that, although our feelings and emotions are useful tools in the search for an out-of-balance characteristic, more fundamentally they play an important role in ensuring that we find our sense of happiness. Many people struggle to understand what really makes them happy, tending to stray into the more familiar but negative attitude of recognising what they dislike or don't want. That's fine up to a point, as it does provide some sense of progress, albeit limited. But rather than walk backwards into our future, as if afraid to see what lies ahead, why don't we just turn around and walk in the direction we're travelling? By applying this simple analogy to ourselves it will help us to gain a lot more confidence in our ability to proceed and reach our desired result of health and happiness.

In order to attain this level of understanding we need to learn how to separate the thoughts in our heads from the feelings, emotions and sensations that we feel everywhere else. Our behaviour is largely governed by how we think, and we're accustomed to surrendering our power to our thoughts. But in order to separate our thoughts from our inner self we need to listen to our emotional voice.

Feelings and emotions are for the most part the only thing we can truly trust. There's no way of cajoling them into giving us false information; they respond dutifully time and again no matter how often we choose to ignore them, preferring our thoughts instead. If we were truly evolved spiritual people we wouldn't need to work things out all the time, we'd instinctively know what was right for us. But instead, we lack trust in our own truths, preferring other people's opinions to our own intuitive self, leaving us at times in a bit of a muddle. Assuming that other people know what's right for us is somewhat rather strange wouldn't you think, when in all probability they'd be speaking from their own viewpoint rather than from ours? If we had more faith in who we are and in our own ability, we wouldn't need continual advice from other people as confirmation of what we already know. We'd just trust our intuition. The less we're influenced by other people's opinions the better off we are.

"A trembling in the bones may carry a more convincing testimony than the dry documented deductions of the brain"
Llewelyn Powers

Going back to the example in the first chapter, our already disgruntled lady, Marjorie, finds it difficult to achieve a friendship with Sophie that doesn't make her feel used.

We've already identified how the imbalance in Marjorie's character trait - weak – will contribute to attracting these kinds of scenarios. Whether it manifests in her friendships or other ways isn't so much of concern as the realisation that she has largely brought this upon herself. We could apportion part of the problem onto Sophie for taking advantage of Marjorie's imbalance if it were helpful, but fundamentally it's up to Marjorie to be responsible for her own characteristic. She needs to learn how to bring herself into balance to avoid repeating her experience. This is an important point and one that we'll come back to again, for life patterns revolve; they replicate and replicate until at some point the lessons are learnt and we can move on to the next module.

It would be wonderful if we could learn more quickly, to enable our patterning to be more fluid and ever-changing. That's what this book is about, to learn under guidance how to improve oneself with greater skill and ability. We can achieve just this by making greater progress in our own self-development, eliminating time-wasting and unnecessary experiences that slow us on our journey.

We've established that Marjorie doesn't realise that what she expects from life is what she gets. She doesn't appreciate that she's responsible for creating this scenario with her friend Sophie – at this stage she only feels the imbalance. Remember, we're not focusing on another person's characteristic to excuse our own behaviour. We're only using it as a way to help us see what is creating the imbalance.

In order for Marjorie to evaluate her feelings about Sophie, she'll need to look deeper. She'll need to step away from her thoughts for a while and rely completely on her gut feelings, reactions and her intuition. We're going to work on a completely feelings and emotional level, where common sense and reasoning don't have a window. This can be harder than you think because we're so used to working things out with our heads that we often ignore any discomfort or communication coming from other parts of us. This technique will be used time and again in our search for balance and freedom as it will help us to attune our non-verbal communications.

Marjorie has explained that she feels she is weak when asked to go to parties with Sophie, but still goes under the pretence that she'll enjoy them to keep Sophie happy. So what's happening on a subliminal level? What is it that her body is trying to convey to her in emotions and feelings that she doesn't understand and so isn't acting upon?

I asked Marjorie to tell me about a time when she was being asked to go to a party by Sophie. Remember, this isn't a one-off incident.

'Sophie rang and assumed that I'd go with her to a party. She said it was on Friday and that there'd be loads of RAF blokes, loads of drink and that we'd stay over at the house of one of her friends whose parents were away.

She just kept going on about how great it was going to be and how drunk we'd get without letting me speak.'

At this point Marjorie began to complain about how inconsiderate and selfish Sophie is. She was frustrated about how Sophie 'knows' she hates this kind of thing, but still makes her go anyway. This is an extremely common response. As soon as we start to feel the imbalance, we focus on the person that we're blaming for causing it, rather than staying with our own discomfort. This is why we remain in the vicious cycle of manufacturing similar scenarios. It's so much easier to focus on other people's perceived faults than our own. If we want to progress we need to remain honest with ourselves by gathering enough information to help lessen the strength of the characteristic that we're working on, with no sense of self-judgement.

So Marjorie accepted that she had flipped into focusing on Sophie's perceived faults rather than being honest with herself, and returned to examining her 'weak' trait.

In order to lessen the effect of this trait, Marjorie needs to understand how it manifests so she can alleviate the weight of it. As we've already explained, the fact that she appreciates that she has the trait and its antonym automatically lessens its weight a little, but now we need to ensure that it's lightened even further so that it has less impact on her life.

First we need to ensure that Marjorie stays grounded: we don't want her focusing on less relevant issues when she feels any discomfort. A simple way to do this is to slip your shoes and socks off and feel the floor beneath your feet. Spread your toes to make sure each is firmly connected to the floor. Notice all parts of the feet that are touching the floor, the temperature of your feet, the freedom from being encased in shoes. Is the surface you're standing on cool and calming, or fluffy and comforting? Once you've focused on these sensations and drawn your awareness away from your head into your feet, you may start to feel a sense of calm wash over you, as if you're altogether more stable. This is because if we remain in our heads too much it can start to feel as if we're a little top-heavy, as if our head is whirling us about with all kinds of unimaginable thoughts and scenarios without a grain of truth. So in order to fix yourself firmly in the ground, imagine now that you have roots starting to sprout out from the soles of your feet. Mentally watch as they grow downwards through the soil you're standing on, reaching further and deeper into the earth with each breath that you take. Once you feel the roots are down deep enough you may like to anchor them as extra security. Imagine a beautiful crystal, a colour of your choice, and wrap your roots around it. Now we're ready to progress with our exploration.

As Marjorie has identified these traits within herself she's already on the route to balance. In order to help her accomplish this, we need to examine even further what aspects make up this trait.

Again, Marjorie needs to do this, as you'll remember it's not our interpretation that matters but what it means to her. I asked her to write a list of every thought, feeling and experience that comes to her mind when considering the word 'weak' in the context she has given. Once this is done she does the same for strong. I have listed them.

Weak	Strong
Unassuming	Pushy
Harmless	Thoughtless
Uneventful	Inconsiderate
Withdrawn	Ungrateful
Unproductive	A bully
Not good enough	Disingenuous
Undeserving of	Unkind
friendship	Hurtful
Victim	Over-opinionated
Wishy-washy	Using
Easily walked over	Ashamed
Used	Unlikeable
Undervalued	Of importance
Ineffective	Falsely happy
Abused	Shallow
Low	Nose in the air
Sad	Brittle

The lists she gave are quite revealing. She realised whilst writing them that no matter which end of the seesaw she was looking at, *neither actually contained the characteristics or feelings that she would want for herself.*

As a gauge to monitor her progress, I also asked her to explain how it felt to be in both positions at this point, and by this I mean within her as sensations and feelings.

Using her grounding technique to ensure her roots were firmly planted in the soil, she confirmed that when she thought about 'weak' her body felt heavy, unmovable almost. It felt bleak, dark and lonely. She felt a pressure on her chest, its strength almost suffocating. She felt tearful.

When I asked her to tell me how she felt when she considered her position of 'strong' she said that it felt higher but not in a nice way – like towering over somebody. She felt distant, as if her body wasn't all there, a bit like a TV channel that wasn't properly tuned in. She felt she was thin, shallow of breath, as if her feet weren't on the ground … almost anorexic, undernourished.

If at any point Marjorie wished to take a break from working on this trait, she could tune back into her body at that point and re-evaluate her feelings and sensations, as we've just done. This gives her greater confidence in what she has achieved already, and a marker to work from next time.

So with the images and feelings very much in mind, we decided to work even further and reduce the strength of some of the characteristics. The aim is to lighten their influence and hence provide her with a far more compassionate and caring position.

We swapped her focus to the antonym – strong. I wanted Marjorie to look at the situation with her mother, not from her perspective but from her mother's. We used another technique to help Marjorie see things from her mother's viewpoint, without overlaying them with her own thoughts and views. This can be somewhat difficult as none of us like to think that others may be unimpressed by our behaviour, but if we're to lighten the effect of these traits this is essential.

People often reflect back things that they *think* are correct or *think* the other person may be feeling. It's much more important to actually try and stand in the other person's shoes and get a true representation of the event from *their* perspective rather than just pretend to because it's too uncomfortable to be that honest with oneself. I use a bit of imagery that I've found to be very effective for this purpose.

Imagine you're in a street with houses on either side. Marjorie lives on one side of the road and her mother lives directly opposite. From where Marjorie is standing she believes that she can see straight into her mother's front window. She assumes that from her viewpoint she's absolutely correct and has no need to wonder if what she sees is how it is. However, her mother has quite a different perspective on both Marjorie's house and that of her own. I ask Marjorie to imagine walking over to her mother's house and to stand where her mother was standing, looking out towards her home. From this position it's much easier for Marjorie to grasp all the feelings and impressions that come to her with the view to lightening her characteristic of strong. As she does so she becomes less 'aggressive' about her mother's requests to meet up and actually becomes quite humbled.

She can now see that the way she was treating her mother was little different to how Sophie was treating her. This is a massive revelation and will help her tremendously with coming towards the middle of the chosen characteristics of weak and strong.

Whichever characteristic you choose to work from, the progress you make on one side will always have a positive influence on its antonym. Marjorie's acknowledgement of her 'strong' characteristic regarding her mother had a direct and positive influence on her position on the 'weak' characteristic that she discussed when talking about Sophie. And that was before we had even started down the road of assertive communication and applying techniques to ensure that her needs were met!

So without puncturing Marjorie's self-esteem any further by elaborating on her *perceived* failings, we've brought her towards the middle and she now views herself very differently. She feels more empowered and more of an equal to Sophie. She feels she has less to prove and is able to meet more in the middle with her mother ungrudgingly ... and believes that she may actually quite enjoy it.

It would be useful to see how Marjorie's seesaw looks now, bearing in mind she hasn't actually done anything yet with regard to changing her behaviour to either Sophie or her mother. We've been working on a purely subliminal level and yet already she can feel that her sense of balance between these two contradictions is appearing.

So, trusting her gut instincts, I ask her to again place her two positions on the seesaw. The grey markers indicate her new position.

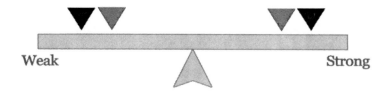

Weak   Strong

Her schematic now looks like this, showing a noticeable difference in how she thinks and feels about herself. She has considerably reduced the weight of each characteristic and as a result increased her level of self-esteem purely by looking at herself more honestly and without self-judgement. This confirms how powerful this method of self-development can be, and what each one of us has the ability to do with very little effort.

EXERCISE

Take one of your own characteristics from the list that you created in the first chapter. When was this characteristic most noticeable? When did it have the greatest sense of power over you? On your own seesaw, and using your intuition as a guide, place an X to represent how strongly this characteristic manifested itself. Repeat this with its antonym, its opposite characteristic, remembering to place the level of greatest influence furthest away from the fulcrum.

Now that you have a visual concept of these two characteristics, you'll have a much better understanding of how to balance yourself.

If you feel ready, make a list under both characteristics of all the thoughts, words, images that you can attribute to each. This will give you a far more rounded interpretation of your characteristics.

Dwell on this

The further we go down the route of self-improvement the further we want to travel.

Section One

Chapter 3 – The depths of friends

In this chapter we're going to look at some of the more complicated aspects within our friendships. By doing so we can reduce the 'push-pull' tendency that can so often happen.

Friends are our peers and our social support network. They fulfil needs way beyond those we're consciously aware of, and likewise we do the same for them. Friendship spans a spectrum of intimacy and openness and as such can be mere acquaintances or best friends.

Even so, our friends are often a source of irritation and disenchantment, and can cause an array of suffocating emotions that aren't so good.

Unlike genetic links (where we've less say in the matter!) friendships are more tenuous. We choose who we want to spend our time with. Perhaps that's why we struggle to make sense of the range of emotions that we experience when their inconsistencies are apparent; it confuses our already sensitive self as we've chosen to be friends with that person in the first place.

So in order to unravel this complication we need to understand how friends can balance each other.

"A friend accepts us as we are yet helps us to be what we should"
Author Unknown

What makes *us* good friendship material? There are times when we misunderstand a situation or feel that we're taken for granted. By combing through the different layers of interaction between ourselves and our friends we can see just how *we* contribute to the confusion. To do this we need to understand what draws us together in the first place, so that we have a point from which to work. *What we're looking for in our friends is a way to balance our own characteristics.*

If one of our jobs is to do the weekly food shopping, how we go about it is largely up to us, just so long as the food appears in the fridge. That's what we're doing here: we're keeping the end goal very much in focus whilst we decide our own route. Just so long as we're prepared to open our minds to this level of development, then we've made some progress.

Exercise

*What makes **you** a good friend? Write down as many characteristics as you wish and we'll refer back to them a little later.*

This is not an attempt to identify other people's perceptions of you, or how they respond to your characteristics. Keep this focused on your own opinions and values rather than being influenced by anyone else. This is a true reflection of who you believe you are without being altered by another's impression of you.

Listed below are some characteristics that you may consider are important when looking at yourself in this way. If you've struggled to identify many of your own, maybe you'd like to select some from this list.

A good listener

Patient

Attentive

Caring

Considerate

Understanding

Supportive

Amusing

Fun to be with

Reliable

Trustworthy

Honest

High Integrity

Loyal

Empathetic

Share similar interests

Positive

Encouraging

Approachable

Interesting

Accepts people for who they are

Attractive

Happy

Adventurous

Wealthy

Social standing

Genuine

The list is endless so use your intuition - it's always your best guidance. Don't be tempted to select things that aren't really true even if you'd like them to be. There's plenty of time to develop them. This is an honest assessment of the facts as they are today. You'll find as we work deeper that your true characteristics, your redeeming features, will come to the fore as you become more balanced.

Now that we've identified some important aspects, we need to understand the influence they have. It could be that we've a tendency to run and hide behind less endearing traits at times of stress, which is fairly common. It's a familiar place of comfort where we're distracted from our innermost truths. But although falling back into negative patterns may seem an easier option at the time, suppressing our true self in preference to this hinders our self-development and growth in the long run.

First of all we need to understand why we feel emotions of frustration, anger and upset with our friends when we've just identified all these lovely attributes about ourselves. I don't in any way pre-judge, but we must bear in mind that the list we've made doesn't take into account the weight each one of those characteristics holds if we're not in balance. And this is the crux of the problem.

Let's take a trait from the list above and expand on it using some case notes from a client of mine, whom I'll call Adam, to help us to understand the influence of 'Honesty' (from his perspective).

Initially we might think that it's an admirable characteristic to have - its meaning is clear and succinct. Who'd disagree with that? But I beg to differ, as with all traits there's a more positive and negative aspect.

If we look at the antonym of honesty, the opposite effect, it gives us a much clearer overview of what we're working with. When asked, Adam said 'Dishonesty'. So we now have the counter opposites to place on Adam's seesaw so that we can work towards a place of balance.

Honesty   Dishonesty

At this point some people may struggle with this analogy as we've placed both traits on the opposite ends of the seesaw in order to bring them in towards the middle. Suddenly honesty has become an extreme, out on a limb, rather than being in a place of balance. So we need to explain how the extremes manifest for Adam to help him understand their influence.

To do this we'll need to appreciate the variances of both characteristics. By placing the ones of least influence nearer the middle, we'll branch out from there to have the weightiest effects at the ends.

I asked Adam to give me varying influences of both traits as he perceived them. I have listed them below.

HONESTY	DISHONESTY
Fair	Little white lies
Straight talking	Cunning/Scheming
Brutally honest	Cheating/lying
Honesty to gain power/ Overtly virtuous to harm	Treachery/Betrayal

We plotted them along his seesaw, placing the weightiest influences towards the extremes so he'd have a good idea of how influential these traits were to him.

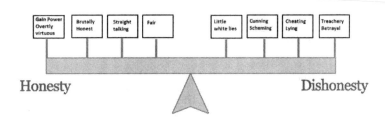

Everyone will have a different understanding of these traits; remember it's only Adam's that concern us at this point. It can be quite hard to pick out just a few words to describe the varying depths of each characteristic. Thankfully we don't need to know them all, the fact that we're aware that they exist is enough.

Going back to the seesaw, Adam plotted where he intuitively *felt* both characteristics were. This is the really exciting bit as it's the first step in lessening the impact a trait has on us – **recognising the trait lessens its power**.

Once Adam has intuitively placed his positions on both sides we can assess the trait's impact.

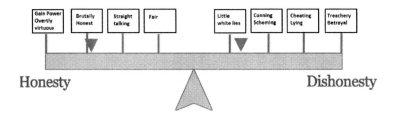

| Gain Power Overtly virtuous | Brutally Honest | Straight talking | Fair | | Little white lies | Cunning Scheming | Cheating Lying | Treachery Betrayal |

Honesty   Dishonesty

From this we can see a huge imbalance. Not only because he's further out on one side to the other, but also from the distance between the two positions in relation to the fulcrum.

This will create a noticeable swing as Adam goes back and forth, first from one side, then the other. He may feel that he does this quite regularly, or perhaps tends to stay in his position of being brutally honest most of the time, flipping over to its counterpart in the lower edge of scheming occasionally. However, the 'honest' position is so much further out compared to the other side that this raises the possibility that Adam *in an extreme situation* has the potential to mirror this furthest point out on the side of dishonesty. This would therefore place him into the realms of cheating/lying or even betrayal, which he's either not aware of or isn't able to accept at the moment.

To achieve balance we need to move the position of one or both of the markers. Of course we wouldn't want to move the dishonesty trait any further out as it would create a greater swing and imbalance and defeat the purpose of what we're doing. So we'll focus on the position he has placed himself on the honesty side.

I asked Adam to tell me what 'honesty' in that position meant to him. He found it difficult to start with, as he didn't like to admit some of it even to himself. Once he accepted that there was no sense of self-judgement, he started to open up:

'I'm always let down by other people because they don't seem to have the same values as me.'

'I feel alone.'

'I find I'm suspicious and try to catch people out for lying.'

'It's hard, it actually feels solid - as if I've set this high ideal for myself and it's a struggle to always keep up with it. It's tiring.'

'I feel a little self-righteous, which I don't like.'

'I feel sad, it makes me unhappy.'

'I feel a tension in my head, like a steel band going around it.'

'I'm straight on to anyone who shows the slightest hint of dishonesty, particularly my wife and children, making them nervous that the slightest thing will be found out and blown out of all proportion.'

'There's tension in my chest as if I'm trying to push something out of it – It feels like I'm trying to force my opinion on others.'

'When I think about how it feels I get the sense that I'm at the front of myself rather than running down my centre, like I'm tipping over.'

Once he'd looked at himself in this way, he realised how unhelpful being overly honest was and was ready to lessen its impact.

I asked him what 'brutally honest' *looked* like to him, to give it an image. 'A whipping stick with barbs on it coming down time and again onto the back of my head.' He felt he was cowering from it, but was being forced to go on with this high moral view even though he wanted to stop and be more balanced and less judgemental of others.

By using this visualisation I asked him what he'd like to do with the stick and he said 'break it in half.' So he mentally grabbed it from behind his head and broke it in two over his knee. He said it allowed his head to be more upright.

Then I asked him about his chest. He said, 'It feels like something is pushing me on from inside my chest, forcing my opinion ahead of me, making me rigid and judgemental. It's the same in the front of my head.' After some thought, he said he wanted to make it into something more soft and pliable. He imagined it first as hard plastic, before allowing it to become softer and more malleable, as if it was being heated up ready to be moulded into any shape that he'd like. Once he'd done this he realised that he had used its rigidity as a way of protecting himself, trying to hide behind an ideal to feel a sense of worth. Having realised this he bravely went on to dissolve it completely in a type of furnace. He watched it turn into melted wax before he poured it down a drain, releasing himself from its influence.

Adam's sense of balance, which he'd felt was to the front of him, had now moved back closer to his spine and he felt more able to relax. Interestingly, he said that he felt that he didn't need to maintain 'the moral high ground anymore'. He felt more 'human and normal and was able to take a full breath'. He said he hadn't felt able to do that for a very long time.

Adam plotted on his seesaw again and amazingly had already brought his 'honesty' marker in considerably (as designated by the grey 2).

We went on to uncover some other aspects to his healing that surrounded this until he ended up with both aspects equidistant from the centre (as shown by the light grey 3).

Don't expect to get both the markers dead on the centre point. Being a short distance apart on either side is great acknowledgment of your work and it'll ensure that your swing back and forth will be far less noticeable.

As with everything we do in this book, we need to be prepared to look at ourselves with honesty and have confidence that we won't be ridiculed for our efforts. If we feel that someone may read our innermost thoughts before we're ready to release them, it could hamper us. For this reason I suggest keeping your notebooks private until such time as you want to show them to someone else.

Below are a couple of examples from some of my other clients. They may help ease any concerns that you have about being so '3 dimensional', by allowing images to help guide us with our work.

Example 1

Carole described how her throat felt tense when she was around small children, particularly her brother's. She saw it as a type of self-hatred that throttled her as punishment for not being able to get pregnant. Once we looked at the trait that exposed this, short-temperedness, she soon realised that this wasn't to her benefit. She was actually harming herself, and becoming bitter and resentful in the process. Accepting that she herself created this disturbance in her energy field made the letting go of it so much easier for her. She mentally untied the knot of the rope that she was throttling herself with, releasing her from all constraints. As a result of this she felt that she could be far more honest with her brother about her feelings about wanting children, without letting her aching disappointment of not having them stop her from enjoying her nieces and nephews.

Example 2

Julie felt that she lacked confidence, most noticeable when at work. She was good at her job but felt the other secretaries were sneering at her behind her back. She chose the trait of 'timid' as the main characteristic to work on, but soon realised, once she started this process, that there were far more dominant characteristics that she was hiding from. She found it quite difficult to be completely honest with herself to start with, but once she unravelled the 'hornets' nest' as she described it, she made rapid progress. When asked for an image or feeling she said 'there are insects buzzing about inside me, making me feel nervous and flighty.' When I pushed her to focus a little more she could see a hornets' nest, but it was constructed with rope rather than the usual papery nests. The old adage about opening up a hornets' nest is very familiar to us, but how often do we stop to reflect on the nature of such beautiful insects; their nursemaid ability and hardworking characteristics are just as important as their stings! By unravelling the rope that formed the nest, Julie was preparing to see the other more relevant characteristics which contributed to her concerns at work, both the pleasant and beautiful ones as well as those considered to be more detrimental to her sense of oneness.

Weight and the sense of suffocation are quite common when it comes to tuning in to our sensations and feelings, as are tight bands around heads and throats. Our images are applicable to us and could be connected to our type of employment, hobby or experiences. An artist may like to work with colours while a doctor may prefer to think in terms of anatomy. But more often they're generic and easy to understand. Don't limit yourself to one interpretation.

Be open to exploring all the little nuances held within the image that you get, rather than sticking to a more linear approach. We're trying to expand human consciousness and as a result we need to be prepared to push our limits in order to progress. Like the example of the hornet, rather than *assuming* it's purely a message about its sting, or more commonly the collective nightmare of unleashing the whole nest upon yourself, please see it as a wealth of invaluable information where the message could be more specific. As in the case of the hornet, it could be as much about warning of pain, short temperedness, being mis-understood, resilient, hardworking, attentive, social ... or the clearing out of a whole load of other issues that are slowing your progress. It's your image; use it to your best advantage.

Exercise

Find a quiet space and allow yourself to focus gently within. Note any aches and pains, emotions or feelings that are present. Think about how hot or cold various parts of your body are. Notice all the parts of your body that are touching a chair or the floor.

Use the rooting technique we mentioned earlier, secure your roots around a wonderful crystal.

Focus on the first trait that you identified earlier in this chapter. Sense its antonym and label up your seesaw, putting each trait on either end.

Take time to give gradations to these traits. Doing this will help you to understand how the different levels manifest. Once you've done so, place an X to mark where you intuitively feel both characteristics' weight hangs on you.

*Focus on the trait that's the furthermost from the centre (should they be equidistant, you can do either). Ask yourself what that position means to **you**. Note down* *every feeling, emotion, thought and experience that surrounds the marker's position, to give as much information as possible about the influence it has on you. Really work hard at this - extract every piece of information so that you can release its weight. Don't judge yourself or have harsh thoughts: the deeper and more honest you are, the better the result.*

By simply doing this exercise, you've already made massive inroads into your self-awareness. If you want to leave it there for now, that's fine. However, if you wish to continue by bringing the impact more towards the centre, let's continue.

Don't worry if you don't get as many thoughts and feelings as Adam, sometimes one or two words or feelings are enough.

Please don't underestimate the power of this exercise: it's hugely beneficial and will highlight other characteristics that you may not have considered before. It could also draw attention to some uncomfortable feelings and memories which may indicate other areas that need to be worked on. However, don't push yourself into exploring these at this juncture, wait until you have more experience, but keep a note of them for future use.

Now that we have a comprehensive understanding of how this trait manifests itself within you, we're at liberty to start to lessen its power.

Allow an image to float into your head that represents this characteristic (whichever end of the seesaw you chose to work from). It may be that, like Adam, you felt different things in different places within your body. If so you may need to work with one area first before going to the next.

With each image decide how you want to release it and then allow your intuition to guide you. Have fun with this, it's amazing how different your images can be!

Dwell on this.

The mastery of conception is the beginning of winning.

Section One

Chapter 4 – Working together

We're going to take a break from our own soul-searching to examine how people complement each another. We've all heard the old saying that 'opposites attract', but do we truly understand such a statement? To do so would benefit our health and progress.

Can you think of a time when you've felt exhausted or irritated when around your family or friends? Has it ever confused you? Or made you wonder why it happens?

Some people may feel physically unwell in these situations. Others can get short-tempered, resentful or even jealous. This isn't how we want to feel around our loved ones, but sadly it happens more than we would like.

These markers, let's call them emotional communicators, are useful in deciphering the hidden message behind these times of angst.

When we ignore the message that these emotional communicators bring, and fail to make the necessary connection, the symptoms tend to increase. It's like turning the volume up on our radio so we can hear. It can leave us feeling stressed, tired and irritated.

Life is about self-development. If we wish to progress to our full potential then we must understand the importance of our emotional communicators. Not only will this benefit ourselves, but also our friends and family. Ego is a strange thing; we deny its existence in us whilst at the same time constantly sparring with it!

A trait or behaviour exhibited by someone else that creates an emotional reaction within us will inevitably be one of our own unbalanced characteristics. As we said before, it becomes an irritant and, although it may manifest in a completely different way or less frequently, it will show itself at some point.

To reduce this irritation and hence its power over us, we need to identify the trait and place it, with its antonym, on the seesaw. We need to ask ourselves if it was easy to recognise. Does it reflect a characteristic that we didn't wanted to acknowledge? Does it manifest as strongly or in a different way?

We tend to mirror other people's tendencies. Whether it's immediate or sometime later, we do so as a way to find our point of balance. It's not just because they display the same characteristic that we do that creates the emotional response. It's because both of us, if *emotionally* affected by this characteristic, carry the weight of both the characteristic and its antonym.

This is an important point. If we don't appreciate this it will be difficult to balance ourselves with those we care about.

Whether it's partners, school-friends or siblings makes no difference. If we're unbalanced, we can't help but go out on a limb to try and balance with their characteristics.

"Your relationships with others are always a direct reflection of the relationship you have with yourself."
Michael Thomas Sunnarborg

It's not always as straightforward as this, as of course there will be times when other factors need to be considered. But as a general guideline, if both parties have the same or similarly weighted characteristics, they'll either come together as a way to balance each other or, if one or both refuse to relinquish the power of the given trait by flipping over to the antonym, arguments can often ensue.

It's easier to show this effect with a case study. I've summarised below part of a session with a client which incorporates much of what we've been discussing in this first section. It's not complete, as there are many other areas that need to be worked on in order to bring her into balance, but it shows just how effective and transformational this therapy can be.

CASE STUDY:

Kate, aged 40, is a strong-minded woman with a responsible job in advertising. She loves her husband, Ken, dearly. He often works late into the evenings, leaving her with the children, George (aged 9) and Emily (aged 11). On the morning of our therapy session Kate had become upset with her children because George had spilt chocolate milkshake down his clean school shirt and Emily had decided to climb a tree just as they were about to leave for school. On the way to school Kate yelled at them, saying that they *needed to take responsibility.*

Kate was also distressed over a dream she'd had the previous night. It concerned a friend of hers. His name was Graham. She'd woken feeling very angry, as she had taken her husband's and friend's advice to not respond to his emails and texts anymore, even though she wanted to tell him how he was making her feel.

They met at University in her first semester. They'd got on well from the start but not in a romantic way. In the

72

second semester, Kate started to go out with someone called Joe and remained friends with Graham. Graham went on to marry a Spanish woman and Kate and Ken would invite his family over for Sunday lunch occasionally. Kate said that she did this primarily to show Graham how happy she was and to get him to leave her alone.

When Graham's marriage failed and his wife went back to Spain with the children, Graham turned to Kate for support. He said that she was his soul-mate and started to become jealous and deluded. He started to call 6 or 7 times a day when he knew Ken was working late or when Kate was at home looking after the children. She told him that she didn't want to be in contact with him anymore and that she didn't consider him to be her friend. This seemed to make matters worse, which worried her husband. He told Kate to stop replying to any of Graham's messages.

Things quietened down for a year or more until she received a text on her birthday. He'd found her on Facebook and LinkedIn (she thinks he didn't know that she could see how often he views her profile).

Tuning in, having used a grounding exercise first, Kate says:

'I feel I'm festering.'

'I'm angry, I don't want to sit back and allow him to stalk me, I want to say something to him.'

'I'm forced to be passive by friends' and my husband's advice.'

Separating her thoughts from her emotions and feelings, she quickly tuned into both to gain clarity:

Head	Emotions
Grow up and deal with it	I'm feeling sensitive. I want to tell him to go away. I want to say it to him rather than simper in the corner like a wet rag

Author's note: This is interesting: if we were to stay purely with her emotional message, we'd be looking at ways to get her needs met to ease the sense of anger and frustration; as it is, she's holding onto these feelings so tightly that it's caused the subliminal message, brought to her in a dream, to get her to take notice. As I explained earlier, we all too often get overly 'heady' with our thoughts and remain governed by them rather than becoming more neutral and balanced. This can be achieved by allowing our emotions and feelings into the equation.

It would be very beneficial to work on why she's so harsh on herself. Her head-based thought to 'grow up and deal with it' and her emotional response '... simper in the corner like a wet rag' feel so uncaring and damaging to her sensitive soul. We addressed this in other sessions.

Kate thought she had various options in response to her emotional message. When I asked her for some she said, 'Arrange a place to meet on neutral grounds so I could tell him honestly how I feel. Speak to him by phone, email him or write a letter. I could explain to my well-meaning friends and husband how being unable to confront him makes me feel.'

Another option would be to draft a letter, giving vent to all of her frustrations, but not actually send it. This has the combined benefit of not only being wholly useful in getting her feelings out of herself and onto a piece of paper or computer screen, but ensures that she doesn't run the risk of inflaming the situation by making contact.

My intuition highlighted that it wouldn't be in Kate's best interest to make contact with Graham again. We already knew that listening to her head wasn't gaining her any peace. We needed to find another way to work with this to lessen the strength of the emotional response without aggravating the situation with Graham.

I asked Kate to tell me what she thinks of Graham so that we could gain a much clearer understanding of the dynamics at work here. This isn't always needed but in this situation it was helpful.

'He's so wet. No backbone. Very clever but no common sense. He's like a jellyfish. Weak. He allowed problems in his marriage at the expense of the children. He wouldn't do anything to help himself. Doesn't stand up for himself.'

In order for her to understand why she feels so much frustration, I explained that the traits and behaviours we see in others that give us an emotional reaction actually mirror aspects of ourselves. She was a little worried about this and so we went on to prove the point.

I asked her for the antonym of 'don't stand up for myself'. She gave me 'assertive' and placed each of them on the seesaw.

Her seesaw looked like this:

Don't Stand Up
For Myself

Assertive

Having placed the respective positions of both Kate and Graham on the seesaw, Kate could see that, not only did they both have the traits with the equivalent weight, but that they each mirrored the other completely. It was quite a shock for her to recognise this.

Then I asked her to list the various attributes of each trait to ensure that she understood how they manifest. (*Remember this is Kate's perspective, we may view these characteristic completely differently*)

Don't stand up for myself	Assertive
Wet	Obnoxious
Weak	Overbearing
Lacking self-esteem	Selfish
Too Acquiescent	Bullying
Whingey	Entrenched
Victim	Maintaining something is right even when it isn't

I asked Kate to list out how it felt to be this far away from the fulcrum:

'Despise myself.'

'Gutless.'

'Cross with other people because they don't get the point.'

'Cross that other people force me to explain things that I feel they should know, but I don't want to say this to them as I don't want to upset anyone.'

'Feel on edge – almost want to get up and walk away.'

'Not taking responsibility myself.'

'Disempowering.'

'Impatient – don't want to deal with it.'

'Arrogance – intellectual arrogance, why do I have to explain this to you, it's really so obvious what has to be done. You're stupid.'

'Childlike – expecting someone else to sort out my problems.'

Author's note: It can often happen that when a client is getting near to the crux of the issue, they tend to blame everyone else for their discomfort as a way to deflect it from themselves. Kate's admission at being cross with people, and irritated with having to explain all this to me, is just a last attempt to avoid facing the truth. A skilled therapist can, with compassion and kindness, steer the person through this moment of concern to gain a great result. This is one of the reasons that I don't suggest that you help other people to work on their traits; it will inevitably lead to anger and upset, and if handled incorrectly could hamper their progress. It's far better to work through your characteristics by yourself or with the help of a neutral person such as a therapist.

I explained an image of the path along the top of a mountain as our life journey from birth to death. I asked her to see that attached to her was an elastic rope connecting her to the end-point ahead. This rope, when put under tension, causes stress, disgruntlement and disease. It's this pull away from her true nature that's causing her this issue. When I asked how she saw herself on that path in that moment she said it felt as if the path was dipping away to her left, that there was no place left for her to go but to follow it downwards.

This is useful as it helps us to understand just how limited she feels when dealing with this situation.

In order to rectify the position, we need to go back to her childhood to dig out the root that started this way of thinking. This will allow us to re-establish a new route (root) back from then. I'm not talking about working on any particular issue or event, but taking a more general view. The visualisation tool that we've used before is really helpful to us now, as it allows us a real sense of what's happening without going into specifics.

I asked Kate to see herself as a child. She immediately saw a child in a nursery wearing a blue dress and carrying a comfort blanket (which, interestingly, she admits that she still has with her now). She didn't instantly think that the child was her, so I asked her to go inside the child and sense how old she was. 'She's three and has brown bunches and is sitting on the floor'.

Now that Kate was connecting with herself, I asked her to look towards the far wall of the nursery and tell me what she could see. 'Two windows, both are shuttered and a door that's closed.'

I asked her to walk over to the windows and open the blinds – she did and said that it was bright and sunny outside. I then asked her to turn around and tell me what she could see in the room – 'A red table and a chair, and a blackboard.'

I asked her to walk over to the blackboard and write her biggest fear – 'Growing up and having to do it all myself, I won't be good enough.'

I asked her how this made her feel and she replied, 'Panicked and sad.'

I asked her to cross out what she'd written and write 'I am good enough.' She felt very determined and continued to write, 'Just you wait and see!'

I asked her if she could leave the comfort blanket on the chair, which she did, and walk over to the door and open it. Outside there was a playground full of children. I asked her what she wanted to do and she said walk across to the other side. I said that with each step she was going to get a year older until, by the time she reached the other side, she'd be an adult.

Once there she walked along a path that had grass on either side. Her children and Ken were there but she couldn't see ahead. I asked her why this was and she realised it was because there was the brow of a hill. I suggested that she walked over the brow and tell me what she could see. 'It's a bit like a fair-ground. There are loads of things going on, some peaceful, some fun, some exhilarating.' They continued to walk towards it and came to a stile. I told her to let the others go over while she waited behind. I explained that there was a wicker basket with a lid to the right of her and to put any remaining characteristics that she had listed under 'Don't stand up for myself' and 'Assertive' into the basket and secure the lid. Once she'd done so she went over the stile and skipped to her family.

Author's note: Kate chose only to put the characteristics from the 'assertive' side in the basket. This could denote a sense of unwillingness to acknowledge that she displayed aspects of assertiveness in her behaviour. By putting them in the basket she was happy to let them go without facing up to this. Or it could mean that she felt more attuned with her true self with regards to 'Don't stand up for myself' and so didn't have any weight from that side to put in the basket. That would be a topic for further discussion. The reason I asked her to do this was to free her for the moment from either trait's effects so that she could see what her future would feel like when she's brought them both right in.

I asked Kate how she felt after the visualisation and she said, 'I feel unburdened and free – lighter, excited at what we're going to find along the path.'

Then, as confirmation to herself, I asked her to plot her current position on the seesaw, marked on the schematic below with the grey triangle.

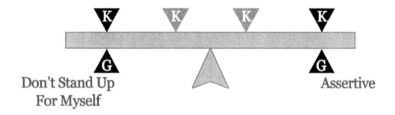

Don't Stand Up
For Myself   Assertive

Kate could now see that she hadn't been taking responsibility for herself. I reminded her of what she had lectured her children about only that morning. Her true nature had been so frustrated at her lack of movement in understanding this particular characteristic, that when she saw it reflected in her children's behaviour, she saw red. She shouted at them to take more responsibility, when she was really shouting at herself.

Of course we can't monitor the effect of this transformation on Graham, we'll just have to trust that it was helpful to him. Speaking to Kate some months later, she said that she'd heard that he'd gone off travelling with a new girlfriend.

In the meantime I asked Kate how she now felt about Graham. 'Fine, I just feel sad for him. I don't need to tell him how I feel anymore.'

This was a hugely important session for Kate and I admire her for her hard work in achieving so much. It's not always as easy to get to the crux of a problem, but Kate's willingness and need to find a solution really helped. But with patience and virtue, and trust in ourselves, we can achieve so much purely by listening to our inner voice. We need to be prepared to be openly honest with ourselves with no sense of self-judgement or remorse.

You can see at the start of Kate's therapy session that she was highly critical of herself, almost loveless. By easing her through this session it helped her to see her path ahead and in so doing, she felt much more peaceful.

As I said earlier, there are still many factors from this session that we need to go back and work on. Why don't you be a therapist and pick out the various aspects that would benefit from some further exploration? Place them on a seesaw, or imagine you're Kate and develop visualisations to aid in her progress.

For now though, Kate is more than happy to move on in her life. It was no mere coincidence that the morning of her session Kate had the dream and the incident with the children to focus her on the issue. She was so excited about how much better she felt that she wanted to go home and tell her daughter about the session. Explaining how friends inter-react with one another as a form of self-denial is a wonderful tool to give Emily to use in life.

Exercise

Identify a time with a friend, husband/wife or work colleague when you felt your energy drain, or had some other form of emotional communication that left you feeling disgruntled or 'off-colour'.

List the main characteristic with its antonym and identify how each trait makes you feel, how it manifests, what thoughts surround it, and list them below each trait. Then plot your position for both aspects before considering the other person's. Obviously this is fairly subjective but trust in your gut instinct to get this right.

Once you've done so, notice where you've placed the weights for both people, it'll be very informative.

One way that we can use this to great effect is when we're having problems in a relationship. Working on our own aspects will automatically lessen the characteristics of the other person, bringing us both towards the middle reducing both our extremes of behaviours and outlooks.

Dwell on this

Arrogance is more a state of self-hatred than considering you're better than another.

SECTION TWO

Section Two

Chapter 5 – Variety

We're creating a framework that now needs some body. How we do this depends largely on personal endeavour, but it's important to consider the following points.

Continuity is a must. We can each make an effort for a short period or over a particular point, but it's the continuation of effort that really counts. It's not about achieving the *best* results every time, it's the forethought and dedication over the duration that brings results.

Initially I struggled with staying power, not because I didn't believe in myself and the benefits of self-development, but because I had a tendency to lose interest. This is a characteristic I've learnt to accept and adapt to be an asset and now my will to succeed is motivated by variety, performance and accomplishment. This is something we'll all come to master as we continue to work on ourselves.

As we develop a keener sense of self we need to keep motivated. The least effective course of action when trying to escape a house fire would be to stand still. Likewise, if our goal is to run a marathon, going to the gym to train calf muscles won't on its own develop our long-distance running skills. Our will to succeed has to be inspired by variety and progress.

Spiritual fitness is very similar to physical fitness: it takes continued effort to reach a certain level and to then maintain it. If we don't sustain our new resolve to improve, we could soon tire or slip back, 'deconditioning' spiritually as a result. Unlike trekking to the gym or pounding the streets though, all we need to do is look inwards.

"Life is like riding a bicycle. To keep your balance you must keep moving."
Albert Einstein

One way to do this is to broaden our outlook - to notice life as if students. If we're prepared to be 'taught' rather than be ostentatious, we'll get so much more from this.

We need to understand detachment in this way as it's a skill we'll use often. It enables us to become more objectively certain and less critical of both ourselves and others. Some may feel uncomfortable with this, preferring to stay very much in the centre of what's happening. And that's OK, it's a choice we have to make and we're not casting any aspersions.

If we want to progress though, the best way forward is to step away from these seemingly delicious distractions and concentrate on our full potential.

Choice is important. By defining the outcome we're providing the blueprint to work from. If we're concerned about getting through a difficult week, then that's the choice and level of investment we're prepared to make. However, if our plan is to become spiritually mature, to expand our knowledge and care of ourselves and others universally, then that's a completely different matter, where lifelong experiences will be set up to achieve it. The *choice* is ours.

We talked about creating experiences in the earlier chapters. Our thoughts, mood and commitment to a project create the timeline to the result. If we can only look to the future in terms of weeks, then that's as far as our experiences in connection with that choice will come about. If, however, we want a lifelong commitment to a project, then we'll realise it with foresight and wisdom, far outstripping anything we've ever dreamed of. It's down to personal choice and we mustn't let anyone else influence this. If it comes from the heart then we'll achieve it, even if it isn't as we first envisaged.

As developing subjects we have the right to choose how far we want this to impact on our lives. It's not a matter of making a decision for life as if it were non-negotiable: we can change our minds at any point, reducing our level of commitment or deciding to really go for it. The choice is ours to make.

So how much do we want from this?

If we're not certain, how are we going to make it happen? The distinctions between human characteristics are complex and take years to fully appreciate. If we think we can master them just from reading the first few chapters of this book, then we're very much mistaken. I'm not saying this to scare you but to highlight the fact that we're developing people and as such will learn the same lessons time and again, but from a higher viewpoint.

Have you ever wished for something but ended up with something completely different? It's a fairly common phenomenon that will catch us out from time to time. It's the wisdom of trust that we'll go on to speak about.

Without a belief in who we are, we often sabotage our interests without realising it. By narrowing our approach we're effectively narrowing our awareness. We'll never fully grasp the magic that surrounds us all if we aren't prepared to be open and attentive, it just won't happen. And to be an example is the most powerful form of choice, in effect an aphrodisiac in the mastery of life and we should never undervalue this.

If we take happiness as an example, a choice or request in life, we may just find we don't get it. This isn't because we're not worthy of such accolade, but for happiness to be apparent we have to look at what takes us to this point, what provides the emotional feedback that confirms we're on track.

Happiness alone is a fairly innocuous undertaking as it doesn't conjure up any parameters to work from. It's an effect, an emotional response that confirms we're going in the right direction and so are in a place of comfort. It's not a standalone request or attainment.

In order to achieve this wondrous state we need to discover what gives us the warm, fluffy, uplifted feeling we desire and then set out a blueprint to follow. What takes any one of us to this point is pure conjecture, as it's down to personal choice, but it's a side effect of becoming spiritually mature, grasping sight of the bigger picture and expanding human consciousness. What we feel we get from life may be something quite different in a year or two when we've had time to take the blinkers off and appreciate how spectacular life really is. If we can have the courage to stand back and assimilate the facts we'll be astounded by how innovative and affirming Life-Changing Moment is.

We all crave happiness and want the best for ourselves and however we dress it up, love, communion of spirit and alignment are the answer to our prayers.

By using the *feelings* of happiness as a guide, we can ensure the direction we're heading is correct. It's not for us to decipher the route for someone else. Likewise, trying to pass the responsibility for our own happiness onto someone else offends, burdening loved ones with hopes and ideals that are impossible to fulfil. Happiness is down to personal endeavour, it's not for others to give. If we truly want success then *we* need to master the response to our own request and stop blaming others for the result. If we accept we're creative in terms of our experiences it will go some way in correcting this. Taking responsibility empowers us and ensures we're ready for the next stage of the journey. Any sense of dis-ease is purely of our own making and it's down to us alone to bring us back towards the middle, the place of comfort where we can achieve oneness and the state of happiness.

So the next time you say, 'It's not my fault' or 'he/she is making me unhappy because …' ask yourself this – why should they be targeted as your source of dis-ease when all about you is abundance and grace? We need to take responsibility for ourselves and make attuning to the highest energy and maintaining our position of growth our prime focus, rather than diminishing its effect with petty-mindedness and poor attitudes.

We need to be caring and considerate of other people's wishes and sensitivities. We're not advocating self-centredness at the cost of others, but we're going to need to take responsibility for ourselves. If we find our sense of self is lacking, we need to devise a way to rectify this.

One way we can do this is by examining the areas in our lives that bring us this sense of happiness - the lovely light, bright sense of contentment and excitement that we wish for, and ensure we attend to each. Often we're not sure what these are, so remain in a cloud of fogginess, looking to everyone else to provide them for us whilst being left with the sense of under-accomplishment. But rather than stay with this veiled approach let's find a way to bolster our own insecurities and gain a far clearer understanding of what contributes to our own happiness. By examining our lives in this way we'll explore the areas that are prone to neglect and start to rebuild them with love, trust and confidence.

The method we use is very simple, but effective nonetheless. Imagine a strip of cine film or the old 35mm camera film stretched across the page to represent a 'snapshot' of our life today. Each frame will signify a different interest or aspect. If we imagine we're trying to encompass our main interests without getting too wordy, it will help us to encapsulate them. What would they break down into?

Don't worry at this stage if it's not complete, we're just using it as a way to get us started. We'll build on it.

I'll use a client's notes as an example.

Tom came to me because he felt his wife didn't understand him. He felt he did everything to provide for her and couldn't understand why this didn't make her happy, and so was considering divorce.

We talked about his attitudes towards marriage and where they developed from. Often we make assumptions from the example of our parents and other people akin to us who aren't in line with our own truths, but fail to realise this.

He explained that his father was 'dated' in his views, believing the man worked whilst the wife 'kept house.' He even chuckled as he told me, describing it as archaic. His brother had had a turbulent marriage that ended in divorce some time back and talked very negatively about its value whenever Tom asked his advice.

So we can see he wasn't best placed to receive balanced guidance from his family, the people he turned to for help.

We talked about this for a while before I asked him to look at his life in terms of fulfilment. We used the model of the 35mm camera film to help with this, placing a different aspect in each frame.

We can see that Tom only managed to fill some of the frames, the others remained vacant.

Although the schematic doesn't reflect this, Tom couldn't see past his work predominance in order to bring more balance. He didn't place any value on the other areas of his life and struggled to see their relevance in gaining fulfilment. He eventually acknowledged that his brother and sister were important to him, albeit distanced, and so gave them a place furthermost out from his main focus, even though there were frames nearer the centre. This is significant and became part of our discussion later on.

In order to bring some balance we discussed each of the frames. Valerie, his wife, appears to be a source of irritation to him.

'She mopes about the place whilst I'm at work and then expects me to take her out when I get home when I'm tired. At weekends she wants to do things like go shopping when all I want is to get ahead with my work, maybe have a kip and watch some sport.'

As you can see he doesn't value his wife's contribution to his sense of fulfilment. He says he loves her but can't stand the whining about him never giving them time together. He actually found it difficult to stay focused on this frame for long as he kept being drawn back to his work. I asked him why this was and he said it was because he saw the 'wife' frame as black and empty whilst the 'work' one was large, white and fluffy – far more interesting.

As soon as we focused on his work frame he instantly brightened and felt more relaxed and smiley. When I asked him to look at other areas of his life, he really didn't seem to see any. His siblings were there in the background but he wasn't too interested in them, and his friends turned out to be colleagues he went to the pub with for a quick drink after work, so they couldn't really be classified as friends.

Using a technique that we talked about earlier in this book, I wanted to separate Tom's thoughts in his head from his feelings and emotions to help him understand why he felt so despondent at times.

Head	Feelings/emotions
I'm successful	Lonely
Nothing else really matters	Rising pressure in my chest that never goes
Family/wife don't get it (how important my work is)	Feeling as if it's all in my head, almost as if the rest of me in non-existent
	All feels quite dark
	Fairly ashamed of myself – how I treat other people

Tom recognised he was very unbalanced, lacking in so many areas that could bring joy and contentment, preferring instead to focus on the one area that he felt sure would give him that sense of fulfilment – his work. Separating his thoughts from his emotions and feelings provided further confirmation that his feelings of being depressed were emotional communications for him to take notice of. He hadn't realised until this point that he was actually feeling lonely.

One of the problems with single-minded focus over a period of time is that the spiritual body becomes a bit miffed at being ignored. This is when Tom's sense of disgruntlement started to occur.

I asked him to look at ways he could bring more balance into his life by filling in the blank frames. Initially he couldn't see the need, but once he started to look at things he used to enjoy, he threw himself into the task wholeheartedly.

In order to trigger this enthusiasm we talked about his past, places he'd visited, things he used to enjoy, what attracted him to his wife, Valerie, in the first place, and so on. It was enlightening for him to realise how so many of the things he used to enjoy had 'slipped' away.

I don't advocate holding on to the past as a form of identity, but to reflect back occasionally can be beneficial. We need to find a happy medium between growth and familiarity. It's a bit like the water in a fish tank: if you changed it completely without first adapting the new water to the temperature the fish are used to, it could harm them. On the other hand, to leave it unchanged for years would mean the water would become rancid and stagnant. To take out measured amounts of old water and replace with fresh on a regular basis will gain the desired result.

This analogy worked well with Tom as he realised the more he craved for oxygen, the more he focused on the one area that he knew could provide it – work, without realising he was struggling more and more to reach the top just to be recognised, so providing him with a sense of self. He hadn't appreciated that all his frames were as capable of sustaining him once he'd revitalised them, giving him a far more balanced perspective without needing to alter his goals at work.

In order to re-energise the other frames he considered ways he could nourish them. He wrote beneath each frame things that interested him.

Family	Travel	Me Time!	Valerie	Exercise	Social Life	DIY/garden
Family meals	Explore Italy	Photography	Cooking together	Golf	Dinner parties	Lay patio
Visit nephews		Read	Theatre	Hill walking	Join darts team	Grow Veg
Ring sister more often		Listen to music				Fix shelf

Now his frames (or should I say fish tanks!) looked quite different. It was noticeable that he changed the 'wife' frame to 'Valerie' in acknowledgement of how important she is to him. He's working on including further frames and expanding on the ones he already has. There are no limits to the number of frames available: variety is the key to life!

Overall Tom feels much more settled and happy now. The rising lump in his throat, which he had experienced for years, has gone since he's been working on expanding his interests, and his wife is more than happy with his transformation. They booked a holiday to Italy and they play golf together at weekends, which is how they first met.

Exercise

Draw a series of frames to represent different areas in your life, and label them.

The central frames are where your primary focus lies. The frames further out can be the ones that you spend less time on. You may feel, like Tom, that there are some that look vacant. That's fine, just so long as you are aware of them you can go back and fill them in later. Use your intuition to guide you to how many frames you'd like.

From a detached stance, having rooted yourself firmly first, review the clip. Tune into each frame to get an overview of what it means to you, then summarise each one.

Once you've made a fair appraisal of each frame, see how balanced it feels. Sit with it for a while and look at areas that may be missing, or are there but feel under-nourished. Make two lists below each frame – one for your thoughts and the other for your feelings.

Once you've done this, fill in any missing gaps and try to ensure you have a good mix of time alone, time with other people, personal relationship, work, exercise, learning, cultural, creative, travel, etc. The list is endless.

When this is completed, work out how you can nourish each frame. You may find it helpful to break each one down further by having sub-frames, e.g., with your 'family' frame you may wish to divide it into children, siblings, parents, or even further by having a separate frame for each person. It just depends on how far you want to go with it.

Make sure you have an eclectic mix of topics, otherwise this exercise won't give you what you truly want.

Dwell on this

Managing our efforts is as much about self-exposure as it is about reverence.

Section Two

Chapter 6 – Repetition of lessons

In this chapter, we're going to examine why our emotions seem continually to come under attack.

Some of our most painful experiences are when relationships with our loved ones become strained. Spiritual growth can help us to understand why this happens. We've already learnt how to balance our traits by using the seesaw model, now we are going to look at how repetition plays its part.

Our expectations and assumptions about ourselves very often distort our view of who we are, masking the degree of spiritual growth we have already attained. However, if we plot our development on an image of a cone, it will help us appreciate what's happening.

For example, we'll assume that we all start at the bottom and progress our way to the top, the pinnacle of success, in a spiral pattern. As we follow the spiral round, we repeat the same lessons on each rotation but from a higher level each time. This ensures our life lessons are learnt from many different vantage points enabling us to move freely to our point of oneness at the top. Due to the nature of the cone, starting off can seem somewhat overwhelming but the further we go up the spiral, the shorter our rotations become, making it appear that we're speeding up our development.

Pinnacle of Success

How far we progress up this pinnacle or cone of success is down to personal endeavour. The further we climb, the harder the decisions seem to be. This isn't because our life experiences become more unpleasant but because our resolve to remain dedicated, honest and focused gets put to the test.

These tests, which at times can be unpleasant, are essential for spiritual growth. Without them it's easy to revert to bad habits and lose sight of the end goal. By experiencing the rise and fall of our spiritual development we're both advancing ourselves and setting a good example for others.

Having self-respect is essential when attempting to ascend the cone. Whilst it's important that we apply the lessons we're learning, dwelling upon and reliving past mistakes is counterproductive. It can serve to anchor us to that point, making it more tricky to move forwards up the spiral. By avoiding self-judgement our confidence will increase and we'll have more trust in who we really are.

It's important that we actively monitor our progress as it's easy to become entrenched in a way of thinking that ensures we repeat the same mistakes time and again. This will continue until we're ready to say, 'Stop, I get it, enough is enough'. It's only then that we truly learn the lesson and can continue up the spiral – our 'cone of success.' The repetition of life's experiences is a way for us to achieve resolution, nothing more complicated than that. When we fail to learn a lesson we're invariably going to experience it again in a less subtle way.

I'm sure you've heard people say, 'It's the same old story, they never seem to learn'. It's these repetitious events that they're referring to. With each experience there's a wealth of additional information running parallel to the main event. But it's the underlying repetition that we need to take notice of if we want to break the cycle.

The purpose of life lessons is to urge us to progress. If we ignore them we'll remain forever confused, repeating similar experiences and so lingering at the same position on the spiral. The fact that we have these opportunities shows us that we're worth the effort and should take advantage of them.

If we allow others who are less developed to distract and divert us away from reaching our goals, we'll effectively be slipping back down the spiral. Very often it is a subconscious way to ease their own discomfort. Our development highlights their own lack of learning and so, as a way to make *themselves* feel better, they try to drag us back down to their level on the spiral. This is quite common, so just be mindful that this can happen.

Now we understand that we create the repetitive cycles to learn from, by taking the lessons on board, it is then within our ability to break the loop, freeing us to move on up the development spiral. Not only will this give us a wonderful sense of release but we'll be honouring our truths in the process.

Love is at the centre of all self-development. Whether it's love of ourselves, our friends and families, or on a global scale, we need to reflect it in everything we do. If we want to make the most of our chance to move up the spiral then we need to have a more universal outlook. As we work on ourselves within, it will have a beneficial knock-on effect on our external world, creating a more optimistic outlook and positive future cycle of events.

Repetition is our recital. It shows us the level we've achieved thus far without over-complicating matters. If we consider that our encounters at present reflect all we've learnt in our childhoods and our life experiences to date, we won't be far wrong. It's very similar to a pack of playing cards: we're dealt a different hand after every shuffle, but it's how we play that hand that really matters.

With this in mind we need to understand dexterity. By using our skills to the best of our ability we're ensuring a winning hand every time, moving further up the spiral. If we don't, then we'll re-route ourselves back to the well-trodden byways of repetition, discarding our hand as of little use.

Imagine the repetitive loop is a footpath that we walk round every day. We'd soon stop seeing the beauty of the place, lost to the familiarity of the surroundings. That's what happens with our experiences. Without intending to, we're replicating similar scenarios to give us a place of comfort. We're staying in the old familiar territory that we *claim* we want to break from. And that's because we're too frightened to move away. The comfort of the repetition is more than just familiarity, it's lack of self-respect. It confirms to us that we're not ready or that we don't consider ourselves worthy enough of such improvement and so we ensure, by way of repetitive cycles, that we *can't* progress. And that's the real nub of this: we reflect our inner belief, which effectively stunts our growth.

> **"We are what we repeatedly do. Excellence is not an act, but a habit."**
> *- Will Durant (commonly attributed to Aristotle)*

The thought of breaking this negative cycle can feel quite scary. Familiarity acts as our nemesis, blocking our route up the 'cone of success,' limiting our chance to reach our full potential.

By remaining fixed on past experiences and fearing change, rather than seeing it simply as a lesson, we're holding ourselves back as a way to justify our reasoning. There's absolutely nothing to be gained from doing this, the most decisive thing to do is to make a liberating commitment to change. Using this positive, more detached state of mind, we'll be better positioned to review the repetitive scenarios that we've been experiencing, be able to compare them dispassionately and then establish the common narrative.

Imagine we're going on a journey by car. By deciding the route before we set off we're effectively dictating the pace we wish to travel at. If we use a motorway we're choosing ease of driving and speed over the more scenic but slower side-roads. By putting ourselves in the driving seat we're taking responsibility for steering the course of our own destiny. The mirrors though are a constant distraction, pulling us away from the road ahead to reflect on the past. Some people may actually turn their heads round to stare out of the back window! If we were to carry on like this we'd soon come unstuck; spin off the road onto the hard shoulder or into the central reservation. Worse still, cause an accident where not only we but others may be injured too.

If we apply this analogy to our life, we can see there's nothing to be gained from looking backwards. If we remain fixated on our past it will define our future, which could cause further distress down the road simply because we were not looking forwards. Whether we're with other people or alone, this distraction from the truth will slow us down, hinder our progress and possibly alter our potential.

We need to learn how to use our mirrors correctly, looking in them from time to time to reflect back on lessons acquired without being trapped by them. Past mistakes and wrongdoings are just that – past. We need to learn from them and let them go so that we can move further up the spiral.

Our experiences are proportionately linked to the amount of effort invested. The emotions, thoughts and feelings we put into replaying the hurts and upsets from the past, whether we're talking about them or churning them over in our heads, will set in place a re-enactment at some point. It can't help but do so as emotional effort and focus create the future. In effect we're getting what we asked for.

Woven within this, of course, are expectations. What we actually achieve may differ from what we intended, purely because we haven't mastered the concept of faith.

But what is rarely recognised is the importance of self-belief. If we don't believe in ourselves and the importance of our life purpose, how do we expect to gain the most from it? Much like going to work; if we don't believe we're capable of a task and we're not prepared to put in the effort to learn, how do we expect to find it fulfilling? It's just the same.

If we remain focused on the past we're essentially staring straight into our mirrors. We'd be paying so little attention to what's up ahead that we'd fail to see the potholes and diversions. With Life-Changing Moment we're going to adjust this view so we're facing forward, using our mirrors for reference purposes only so that we can concentrate on our futures.

The repetition of experiences, whether we're aware of them or not, are all part of self-development. We create them for ourselves. The distractions that befall us are of less importance as we move up the spiral. But by recounting an event we're reconnecting with the same energies which hold us back. We need to stop doing this and look to our futures.

As we progress up the spiral we'll come to realise that developing ourselves isn't as simple as working on a single strand, it's a whole collection of them. If we think of a bundle of optical fibres, each fibre contains and transmits light along its length. If we don't keep the bundle together some of the individual fibres may become distorted and bent out of shape. This won't necessarily block the flow of information along their length (obviously depending on how out of shape it becomes), but it will lose the illuminating effect of the bunch when held together.

By ensuring our bundle of optical fibres remains in good condition it will allow the light being passed down each strand to reach its destination.

If we imagine that each fibre in the bunch represents one of our lessons, it provides a good analogy. The more we repeat a lesson the more battered our fibre optic becomes, until it flops to the side, like a wilting flower, trying to pass information along its length without distortion.

This is what happens to us. The more we are distorted by the repetitive cycles, the longer our learning is going to take. The light within us will start to fade as it struggles to penetrate the stagnation of energy, we might even lose an opportunity to grow.

In order to rectify this situation and encourage a healthier attitude, we need to return this optic fibre back to the bundle. This requires us to be completely honest with ourselves and take responsibility for our own self-development. There's no place for egotistical behaviour or harsh judgements on ourselves - or anyone else for that matter - it's *our* will to succeed that matters.

The wonderful sense of detachment that we talked of earlier is very helpful here. It will enable us to gain an honest overview and interpretation of what's happening, so that we can free ourselves from the muddle of repetitive cycles.

When we reconnect with the energy of an event we're re-fuelling the experience, giving out the message that we want more of this. The amount of emotional energy we invest will decide the level of the resurgence. It's no different if we want something nice, except that we usually focus our emotional strength on negativity, and so don't focus nearly so much on gaining positive experiences. By continually reconnecting in this way we'll create a blueprint for further experiences of the same ilk to follow.

In the first section we discovered that emotional communicators are incredibly powerful. They are our true inner being's expression of self and come to us by way of feelings, emotions and sensations. If we learn how to interpret them it gains us a huge advantage over negative experiences. But we tend to confine them to the level of subliminal activity.

As emotional beings we need support from friends and loved ones and I'm the first to acknowledge this. However, we need to observe when the scales tip from beneficial to detrimental.

The repetition that we've talked about is the re-emergence of a lesson. By speaking and thinking about it regularly we're giving it power to re-enact itself, entrenching us in the same negative loop. Not only does this deflect us from learning the lessons involved and stop us from moving up the spiral, but it gains us a level of attention not befitting our status.

Often, when we're describing an upset we can inadvertently identify the problem or the solution without realising it. We're so caught up in the drama of the event that we don't notice we've said it. When we're less guarded because of the emotional turmoil we're in the words tend to tumble out. This allows the truth to trickle in. Listen to yourself or your friends at times like this and hear the truth hidden amongst the conversation. It's truly amazing.

Let's look at an example.

Simon uses a dating agency quite regularly. His search for love seems to be constantly interrupted by like-minded women wanting to take advantage of his generosity. Once he realises this, he ends the relationship as a way to preserve his bank balance. What he doesn't appreciate is that his attitude towards money and his mistrust of women keeps him in this repetitive cycle. It ensures that he creates similar situations to prove the point, effectively stunting his progress up his spiral.

In order for Simon to change this pattern so that he can create a better environment from which to meet new people, he needed to step away from his cavalier attitude and appreciate the dynamics involved.

We looked at his characteristics in order to bring them into balance. There wasn't just one, so we made sure that we identified them all and how they imprinted on his personality. He realised that his acrimonious divorce some years back had triggered his distrust of women when it came to his finances. His own insecurities ensured that he developed repetitive experiences to prevent him from emotionally committing to a new relationship. It was much easier for him to blame the women he met than face the truth in himself.

We used a visualisation, similar to the one in Kate's session, to help him overcome the negative effects of his divorce, allowing him to move further up the spiral.

The important point for Simon was to focus on his future, to forge new pathways and gain new experiences that allowed him to grow and progress. By preparing to step off the familiar cycle of mistrust that he's clung to for so long, he'll gain more self-belief and will see women in a different light. By moving up the spiral he'll attract like-minded people who won't wish to take advantage of his generosity.

In the past Simon had jumped to conclusions as a way of ensuring his *expectations* weren't proved wrong. He manufactured situations to make sure this happened, creating a self-fulfilling prophesy. He needed to bring the reasons for this into balance so that he could move away from such negative behaviour and see the truth when he next dates.

Exercise

Identify some repetitive cycles in your life. If you find it hard to see them for yourself, ask a good non-judgemental friend to help you. You'll need to spend some time with this as it won't always be instantly obvious that experiences are connected in this way, and you have a lifetime of them to sift through.

Trust your intuition. If a memory comes to you, it has done so for a reason. Keep a note of it in a journal and, once you've gathered enough, try to identify the themes. For the most part we'll be working on one or two main lessons but there will be other lesser ones that are also worth identifying.

As with all self-development, the moment we become aware of the lesson, we've already started to lessen its influence. Take the first one that you've identified and, from a place of detachment, metaphorically look all around it. Try hard to understand the depth of the lesson. There could be several lessons within one repetitive cycle, so look out for this. Don't be self-judgemental or apportion blame, do this from a dispassionate vantage. The more honestly you can do this, the more honest the information you'll gain. Further learning means further progress up the spiral. We're not worried about anyone else's point of view or lessons, just pick out the strands that are relevant to you.

Having identified this information, determine to change. Be aware of your thoughts. By altering the amount of energy you give an experience, whether it's by talking about it less or consciously thinking about something different when it comes into your mind, you'll be able to disconnect yourself from the negativity involved. This will help you to stop creating the blueprint for further experiences of the same ilk. You will effectively be shutting the gate to the well-trodden footpath that you've been walking and choosing another more virtuous experience higher up the spiral.

Nevertheless, there's no point in doing this if you haven't identified all the learning from the experience. The message will fester inside. Much like putting a sticking plaster over an un-cleaned wound, it won't help it to heal. So before you close the gate to a particular lesson, make sure that you've gained all you can from it.

Dwell on this

The further we move up the spiral the more similar the experience

Section Two

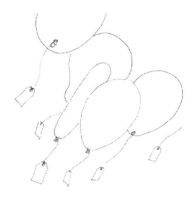

Chapter 7 – Letting Go

Letting go is one of the harder aspects of spiritual development. Whether it's letting go of a loved one who's passed away, or a friend we've outgrown, it can be a hugely difficult and painful experience.

Many of us try to maintain a reasonably good circle of friends. It's nice to do so. But have you noticed how often other people's friends become a cause for consternation to them, upsetting them or allowing them to impact detrimentally on their health or sense of well-being?

With Life-Changing Moment we want to move away from this kind of scenario to make our friendships more wholesome. A way to do this is to understanding the dynamics - the interaction between us and our friends when giving and receiving energy. I'm not going into specifics, as that would take too long, but shall provide an overview and ways to address an imbalance.

We all have the tendency to draw more needy individuals to us, particularly as we become more spiritually mature. It's an effect, much like the attraction of a moth to light, which isn't always welcome. By neglecting our spiritual prowess, we're attracting these people as a way to stunt our growth. In this chapter we're going to look at ways to stop this, so that our friends don't become a burden and we don't feel an obligation to them.

We're going to do this from a point of non-judgement of course, as we're not assuming anything about another person's characteristics. But if a friendship feels too one-sided, uninspired or disrespected then it's time to give it a review.

The seesaw is a very useful tool in helping us identify the imbalances between friends. But we need to be careful who we spend our time with, as friends can imprint on us negatively, suck our energy or manoeuvre our way of thinking more in line with theirs. We are free spirits and have our own characteristics to consider; if we're not able to be who we want to be, then the people that hold us back do so for their own benefit and aren't worthy of our friendship.

This may sound rather harsh but we need to be honest. If a friendship has become too one-sided or detrimental to our health then we need to make a decision either to let it go, allowing more nutritional experiences to come to us, or to re-evaluate and re-affirm the friendship by bringing it more into balance.

"Letting go gives us freedom and freedom is the only condition for happiness."

Thich Nhat Hanh

Once we've done so we'll get an emotional response. This is the *effect* of the movement: it may manifest as tears, euphoria or something quite different. How it appears isn't of concern just so long as we recognise its significance. This effect confirms we're making progress, that we're coming more towards the middle where our sense of purpose and truths are becoming a part of us on a daily basis. Truly wonderful!

As we acknowledge this we'll also come to realise that we're more spiritually compatible with like-minded people. Our levels of compassion and awareness are increasing whilst we're keeping motivated to continue with our studies.

If we limit ourselves to stay with what feels comfortable though, we won't always make the most of this. This is because duality (balance), which is at the heart of all spiritual development, will remain at some level. It may not be as influential as it was but it won't completely disappear until we come right into the middle. And this won't happen if we're not prepared to honour and sacrifice in the name of self-worth.

None of us are meant to stay *in friends* for ever; it can happen and when it does it's good. But it's not a requisite for life, and particularly not if it's detrimental to our growth. Whether we're travelling to the same place or not, we need to know the direction we're heading in case we need to turn off at some point.

It could be that we need to alter the pace at which we're travelling - speed up, take a break or ease back a bit. This is of no consequence as we can always meet up again once we've had time to move further up the spiral.

Whether our reasons for wanting to change the dynamics of a friendship are for spiritual growth, self-preservation or some other hidden facet, it must be done with compassion and love, and the aim should never be to hurt someone or show disrespect. That is not acceptable. We need to allow ourselves space to grow, in fact it's essential if we want to reach our full potential, the pinnacle of success.

So we've accepted that we're all on a life journey and therefore need to respect ours as much as everyone else's. There's nothing to be gained from being belligerent, we need to work compassionately. If we maintain a level of detachment it will help, not only because it will help us understand the dynamics at work but because it will make the whole process seem less *personal* and, as a result, less painful if we want to change things.

When there's disquiet or upset between friends, we need to understand the reason. There's no point in making a friendship work just for the sake of it. It has to be mutually beneficial. We'd make far better use of our time and energies by considering its purpose, acknowledging any help in bringing us lessons and letting go of any aspects that don't serve us so well. By doing this we're respecting our journey and theirs. We won't be clinging to old patterns by preserving outmoded friendships and we'll allow each other to grow.

Letting go isn't an easy option, but it's essential for personal growth and spiritual development. If we allow someone to imprint on us negatively we bear equal responsibility for the fact ... and maybe more.

As much as we'd like to give our all to our friendships, if we're being pulled from the middle, our point of focus, then *we* need to correct it. No one else will. It takes honesty, determination and self-respect to realise this and act on it accordingly. Addressing an issue once may help in the interim but it won't always ensure a happy result. We need to be prepared to keep working at it to bring it into balance so we don't slip back into the old ways. We're creatures of habit and as such need to make sure that we're not forging new repetitive cycles in the process.

People are drawn together for a variety of reasons, far too many to list here. But we're interested in the deeper, more subliminal levels where our subconscious is working for us. When people meet they effectively create a link between themselves, much like a swing bridge. It creates a way to relay information to one another. This is because we're part of a universal web where information is passed between us, much like the internet. If there's a past life connection to be 'repaired', or a skill or lesson to be 'pulled through', it's at this level it will take place.

Detachment and discretion are paramount; I can't stress this enough. If the connection isn't right or the bridge doesn't feel safe enough then why step on it in the first place?

For the most part we overly complicate matters; we fret about what people might think and try to make it work or come out on top without realising there's absolutely nothing to be gained by doing so. We simply need to adjust our point of view and step away, if that's what's required, find a new connection or gain a better sense of self. There's no need to make a fuss. We need to be honest and people will soon come to realise the sense in it. None of us likes to waste our time, it's far too precious and we'll all appreciate the respect this gives.

If we go back to the reason for our self-development in the first place, we'll remember it was to achieve oneness, the centre of all knowledge and grace. It makes absolutely no sense then to take every side road and diversion possible when we're trying to navigate a direct route.

And that's what this chapter is about - no amount of stress or incompatibility will make the connection right. If we learn to accept this we'll have better and more fulfilling relationships.

Bear in mind that not all friends will distract us, for the most part they're great. It's just the few that cause friction, drain our energies or make us feel less good about ourselves that we're concerned with here. These are pseudo-friendships and either need to be rebalanced or weeded out.

Often, people are looking for a safety net, someone to run to when things get tough. They use us as a metaphorical doormat to wipe their weightier characteristics on to make themselves feel better without considering how it affects us. Whatever our reasons for attracting these kinds of people, one thing's for certain: they're doing us no good.

If you think I may have contradicted myself here, you could arguably be right, as developing ourselves does benefit others. But it's the way we go about it that's important. If we can't instigate the ripple effect we're effectively frozen. In order to progress we need to stay focused on our end point, redress any imbalances and free ourselves to be at one with the universe, otherwise no-one can benefit.

Much like the analogy of the oxygen mask in an airplane, we need to put on our own first before we try to help anyone else. This is selfless teaching, not selfish; we're not thinking of ourselves at the expense of others, we're including them in our development to a place of oneness.

For this reason we need to understand who drains our energy and makes us feel less good about ourselves, and who doesn't. This technique will allow us to see without clouding with sentiment, and help us to make the necessary adjustments. Don't worry if it shows an imbalance, we don't have to end a friendship as a result: it's just an indication of a disparity between giving and receiving. Once we have this information we can decide what to do about it.

We're going to use a spider-graph. It will give us a definitive overview without being caught up in individual dynamics. We can go on and use this information in many ways, but for now we'll just use it to identify the exchange in energies.

Drawing from a case study, Lisa had several friends she wanted to include on the spider-graph. With each link, or swing-bridge if you like, the quantity of arrows indicate how much energy she feels she gives out or receives in. This is down to personal perspective, of course - we're not concerned about her friend's opinions. The more arrows, the greater the intensity and investment of energy. Again this isn't meant as a way of casting aspersions on anyone, it's just an honest assimilation of the facts **as she perceived them.**

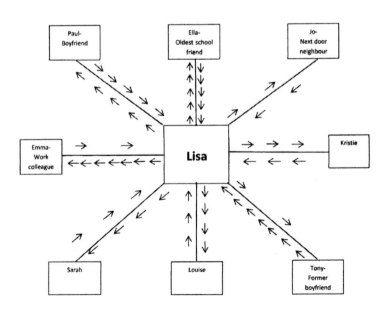

From this we can see that, for the most part, her friendships are balanced. Louise and Sarah could be brought a bit more into balance, but she wasn't overly concerned about them. However, Emma, her work colleague, and Tony, her former boyfriend, showed quite another story.

It transpires that Emma has a tendency to be very needy when around Lisa. It's not so apparent when she's working with the rest of the people in the office, but when Lisa and Emma work together, which is quite often, Lisa feels she has to keep covering Emma's back, protecting the team from her sloppy mistakes. Outside work, Lisa feels she's the mainstay of Emma's social life. She tries to include her in most things but feels a bit resentful that Emma doesn't seem to make any effort to develop her own friendship circle.

In contrast, Tony has a soft spot for Lisa and will do almost anything to help her. He hasn't had a girlfriend since they split up last year and she feels that he's biding his time until she and Paul finish, with the hope of re-establishing their relationship.

We can see from these two examples that Lisa has to focus on balancing these energies as a way to preserve her own sense of self. It's all well and good leaning on a friend for support occasionally, but not if it's going to develop into a continuous loop that doesn't benefit anyone.

We can use the spider-graph to include family members, acquaintances and colleagues - anyone that we give our energies to or likewise receive from. It's not always going to be the case that we're giving more, as with Tony, it could be that we don't make enough effort or tend to lean on someone too much. It's a useful exercise to repeat on a regular basis as things never stay the same for long. If we're not observant we could become unbalanced or drained without realising it. It's a bit like checking the oil regularly in our car, if we didn't we could suddenly find ourselves with a very expensive problem to sort out!

So now that we have an overall picture of Lisa's friendship circle, what are we going to do about it? Recognising it may be enough. Like identifying the traits on our seesaw, by being aware brings us in a touch. But more has to happen if Lisa wants to ensure that her friendships are open, honest and balanced, after all that's the purpose of Life-Changing Moment, to make our lives more universally nutritious.

So the next stage is to take a friendship that isn't balanced, bearing in mind that it's the effort she *feels* that she gives out or receives in that's important, not how others may perceive it, and work it to be more nutritious.

We put both Lisa and Emma on the seesaw, not to balance a particular characteristic, but by way of monitoring progress.

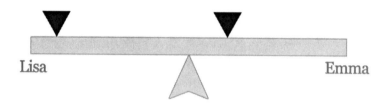

Lisa   Emma

Having done so Lisa considered all the ways she felt her energy was being 'given to' or 'drained' by Emma, and gave them a score out of ten (ten being the most possible, one hardly at all).

Because Lisa feels her friendship with Emma is unbalanced from two perspectives, work and social life, we separated them to make it easier for her.

We started by looking at the work perspective. Lisa made a list of how Emma drains her – imagining it much like a metaphorical sink that she was trying to find the right sized plug for. We often accuse other people of creating a situation when in fact it's our own lack of a sense of self that's responsible. By identifying the various ways that Lisa feels Emma draws on her energy we can gain a much clearer and more honest appraisal of what's going on in order to change it and give Lisa the relief she needs.

Lisa listed them out easily; she was more than ready to release this pressure.

'I'm always her confidante, no matter what the issue is - 5/10'

'I'm always watching her back in case of mistakes – 8/10'

'People think we're inseparable - 3/10'

'She holds me back - 6/10'

Lisa wants to gain promotion but feels unable to try, as she feels stunted by Emma. She said, 'It's annoying that people make silly comments about us being inseparable, but I can handle that.' She finds it tiring and frustrating that Emma constantly relays bits of office gossip to her when she's not interested, and that she has a tendency to embellish for effect.

From this Lisa detected various characteristics that would benefit from being placed on the seesaw, to bring them more into balance. Before doing so, it would be useful to know whether she wanted to improve the friendship or let it ease away (it would be difficult for her to let go completely as they still have to work together)

Using detachment, Lisa gained a good overview. She could have imagined watching herself on a TV screen, but she chose to use a technique which allowed her to rise higher. If we stand on a chair, our periphery view is limited. If, however, we look down from the top of a building, our range of vision is much increased. This is, in effect, what Lisa was doing. By allowing herself to rise subliminally, by using a deep meditation which I led, she could see from a far greater perspective.

From this position, Lisa gained a much clearer understanding of what she wanted to do. 'I don't want to carry Emma anymore, if she messes up, that's down to her. I'm going to try for promotion, and may even do a sideways transfer. It'll be good to get experience in another department.'

It isn't going to be easy at first as Lisa will still see Emma at work, but her will to succeed in her career will motivate her. Emma may find it difficult to adjust at first, so we need to make sure that we ease the friendship apart compassionately, it wouldn't be kind to leave her feeling stranded.

To do this we'll use an image that Lisa can re-energise every day by focusing on her new intentions. It won't resolve the whole issue but it will go some way to correct it. Lisa may need to speak with Emma at some point to explain how she feels, but for now this is a much more gentle approach.

I asked Lisa to draw two circles - one to represent her and the other Emma – letting them overlap to symbolise how intrusive she feels the relationship is. I expected her to use a Venn diagram but instead she drew this.

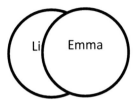

This indicated a hugely *pressing* concern as, not only did Lisa feel she was losing her identity by her name being all but covered, but she couldn't see past Emma to her own future. In an instance she saw how overpowering Emma could be and how urgently she needed to be free from the weight of her.

I asked her what she'd like to do and she said, 'Separate the two circles, put them as far apart as I can.' She wanted to break the friendship. But before allowing her to do so I needed to ensure her mental preparation was correct. She needed to *release,* or let go, as she performs the task. She also had to consider Emma, it would be heartless not to do so. We agreed to separate them and place them a certain distance apart without making it too obvious. This way they could stand beside each other as work colleagues with no sense of resentment or upset. If at a later date Lisa wanted to alter this she could.

Before re-drawing them on the paper, I asked Lisa to start to mentally separate the circles, to give real power to what she was doing. She said she couldn't; it was as if they were stuck together. As she tried to prise them apart she could see a glue-like substance linking them, drawing them back together every time she tried to pull them apart, making it difficult to separate them.

I asked her what she'd like to do about this and she said, 'Dissolve away all the glue.' So in her head she saw herself doing just this, cleaning either side of each circle as if they were coins, before placing them back down. Then I asked Lisa to forgive Emma, to release all negative thoughts surrounding her so as not to create another link between them, to let her go with love, to mentally thank her for her help in bringing lessons to her and to wish her well. Now she felt able to draw their new positions.

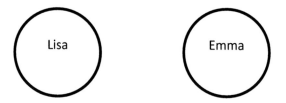

I asked Lisa how she felt now and she said, 'Liberated! As if a great weight's gone from me. I don't mind that we've got to work together, I'll just do my own things and she can do hers. I don't know why it's taken me so long to do this!' She became buoyant and smiley, much younger in her outlook and less stressed-looking – it gave her an instant facelift!

It's important that for a while Lisa checks back in on this visualisation to ensure that it remains as she would wish. I suggested every day for the first few weeks until it becomes 'natural'.

There was little point in doing the same from the social life perspective as Lisa had already made a decision. However, and this is hugely important, Lisa needs to take all the learning from her friendship/work relationship with Emma. There's no point in going through all this if she has to repeat the same experience to learn the lesson. She'll need to go and look at all the characteristics involved and place them on the seesaw to bring them more into balance.

It hasn't gone unnoticed that her spider-graph showed Tony in the opposite position. What Lisa gave to Emma, she took from Tony in terms of energy. This dichotomy needed to be balanced in order to ensure she doesn't create similar experiences as a way to achieve balance with him. Although she was less willing to accept this, she came to see the sense in doing so and has now developed a far more balanced friendship with him.

Lisa plotted herself and Emma again on the seesaw (grey triangle). She's happily confident that it won't take long before she'll move them even nearer the point of balance with regard to her friendship with Emma and already feels less angst about the whole thing.

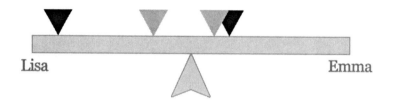

Lisa   Emma

Another consideration that she identified from her spider-graph was her friendship with Ella, her oldest school friend. Although balanced in the energies given and received, she felt it was too much for her now. She recognised the need to let some of the intensity of it go, yet still keep the balance. She realised that the friendship hadn't been allowed to develop as they had grown emotionally, so she decided to loosen the grip on it, maintaining a more mature outlook.

Exercise

Draw up a spider-graph and include on it all the people you give energy to, whether it's family, friends, work colleagues, etc. Draw in a series of arrows to represent the amount of energy you invest in each person. The more arrows the greater the intensity. Then do the same the other way to demonstrate the amount of energy you feel each person gives back to you.

Study areas that show an obvious imbalance and segregate them for further analysis. You may feel that you want to use arrows of different thicknesses, lengths or colour to provide further depth to the analysis. How you choose to use this is entirely up to you, just so long as you understand its significance.

If you wish to expand on this a little further, look at the people who receive a high input of your energy, even if they do reciprocate in return, and consider whether you wish to change this. Do you want to reduce the intensity of the friendship, bring it into balance or let it go?

Is there a noticeable reversal of energy being reflected between two or more people on your spider-graph, as in the case of Emma and Tony? What aren't you being honest about or wanting to face?

If you're ready to, take a friendship that's not balanced and list all the ways that you give your energy, giving them a score out of ten (ten the most and one the least). If you wish you can plot before and afterwards on a seesaw so you can monitor your progress.

Dwell on This

The purpose of friendship is to enhance our sense of self, not drain us of our resources.

Section Two

Chapter 8 – Forgiveness

In this chapter we're going to look at the importance of forgiveness. By releasing the past with love and compassion we're effectively bringing the place of alignment closer to us.

There's nothing to be gained by not forgiving. This is the single most important point. If we wish to do battle let it be about something more purposeful. With all that we're achieving through this book there's absolutely nothing to be gained by holding on to our past hurts or grievances as a way to prove a point. Every hurt can be healed if we allow it. By reconciling our pasts with love we're effectively bringing the full attraction of forgiveness to us. This is such a wonderful moment, so let's not make the fear of releasing stop us from making the right decision.

Some people shudder at the thought of forgiving because they're afraid of being considered weak. Others just simply fear the whole concept. We're told by the major religions that it's the solution often without being given the tools to achieve it. Whatever our reasons for this pause in our evolution we can change it as soon as we acknowledge the need to. Life-Changing Moment isn't able to forgive for us, as it's down to personal endeavour, but it can remove some of the ambiguity surrounding the misconceptions associated with it to help us move forward.

Forgiveness isn't about forgetting. It's about achieving balance through recognising that we each carry the same characteristics and so are similar. They may manifest differently from person to person, but fundamentally we're no different. If we put this into the melting pot we'll come to realise how pointless apportioning blame really is. Human characteristics alone don't cause the break in our ability to forgive, and, as with all aspects of self-development, other factors need to be considered, but, if we can get used to seeing the inability to forgive as a form of self-denial, we'll understand how it stops us our progress.

How we allow these characteristics to impress on us is largely down to individual perspectives and learning. It's not down to any one of us to determine another's reflection, and likewise we're responsible for our own. If we can't appreciate this how are we going to move on?

To forgive is such a worthwhile endeavour. It takes us from the mould we've placed ourselves in, apportioning blame and feeling resentful, and releases fear and any pain embedded within it. You hear of people who have forgiven their captors or murderers of their children because they have faith - faith in eternal justice and/or a greater belief in what's right for them. They don't hold anger, blame, bitterness and resentment as a form of punishment for those who've caused the harm. They move on further up the spiral towards their pinnacle of success.

And this is the level we're going to focus on. We're equipping ourselves with the knowledge of how to forgive, without concerning about what other people might think of us. A truly freeing scenario.

We each are responsible for creating any on-going pain by refusing to forgive and let go with love. We'll come to see the experience as an important life lesson rather than a curse to hold ourselves back with. If other people are incredulous about this, let them be so: their time will come when their lack of learning will be challenged, causing a stunt on the spiral. But for now we're concerned with our own self-development and understanding of forgiveness so we can progress.

Part of the reason people struggle with the idea of forgiveness is that they feel it's a 'cop out', that there's almost a conspiracy to let the perpetrators *off the hook* rather than make them pay for any damage or hurt that's been caused. This is understandable up to a point, as people have to be honest in their approach, aware of their misgivings and responsible for the effects. But that's where the comparison ends. If we don't learn the lessons and let go of the past we're in danger of contributing to the muddle that we're accusing other people of creating.

If we spend our lives looking backwards, bitter and intensely resentful of some wrongdoing, how does that help us? If we all share the same characteristics, how can we justify them in such a manner? Surely it would be counter-productive?

And this is the level we're going to consider.

We're all developing people and by definition aren't perfect but there's no sense of self-judgement involved. We're all capable of harming someone else when there are options not to do so. But by bringing our character traits nearer the centre of our seesaw we'll be able to shake off any incongruence and see from a more compassionate, less egotistic perspective.

Have you ever done something hurtful or inconsiderate to another person that you've not liked yourself for? It would take an extraordinarily balanced person to say no and that's because we all make mistakes. We all have our lessons to learn and how they play out for us is down to individual choice.

We're not apportioning blame here; we're acknowledging that we're responsible for our own experiences and how much we want to gain from them. If we determine to remain on the repetitive cycle of pain and upset then that's for each of us to request, but to respect ourselves and appreciate human consciousness at this level would be much more beneficial. We should *reflect on our own misgivings rather than those of everyone else.*

There are times when the 'crime' seems disproportionate to the lesson gained and that's because it's become more *personal;* it's reflecting at a level far deeper than we're prepared for. But if this is the case then we need to accept it: maybe we wouldn't have learned this lesson any other way. By accepting forgiveness as part of it we're effectively saying we don't mind the form the lesson has taken and won't blame the other person for their part in bringing it to us. We could even go as far as thanking them for their help but this is for when we're further up the spiral.

By accepting those times when lessons have been harsh we're also accepting that the feelings of damage to our soul are illusory. We're by our very nature forgiving, it's just we've forgotten how to be so. We can recover from the negativity incurred purely by realising this and putting forgiveness into practice. We are extraordinary people.

I met an elderly woman once in a hospital A&E department. I was there with a friend who was waiting to have an X-ray. She was wracked with guilt over something she'd done in her life but didn't expand on it. She had fallen and broken her hip, was in a lot of pain and seemed very frightened. Her cries for someone to help her attracted my attention as she lay on a trolley in a corridor awaiting treatment. She was drifting in and out of consciousness due to the morphine so our conversation was brief, but as soon as I stood beside her and held her hand she looked up at me and told me that she'd done some awful things in her life. The sorrow in her eyes was tangible; she'd reached out in a moment of desperation to release the most dreadful of pains she'd been carrying for many years, not to ease the pain of her recent injury.

This happened at a time when I was working on the spiritual concept of forgiveness for myself. Suddenly laid before me was the true magnitude of remorse and the damage incurred by failing to forgive. This wasn't about forgiving someone else though, she was way past apportioning blame, it was about forgiving *herself*. It was an unforgettable moment.

To be able to forgive is an immense gift. This woman had spent years not knowing how to release the burden of remorse from herself, nor recognising the importance of self-forgiveness or believing herself worthy of it. I told her she was forgiven and that she needed to forgive herself. It was a hugely emotional moment for both of us.

But this goes to show just how detrimental non-forgiveness can really be. It eats away at the heart of us, overshadowing our real potential. Whether it's forgiveness of ourselves or others makes no difference, it all comes down to the same in the end. Continually tormenting ourselves with guilt or accusations is a negative cycle that gets us absolutely nowhere.

Forgiveness isn't about letting people off the hook as if saying it doesn't matter - it's about forgiving them so we can all move forward. The woman in the hospital cared more about those times in her past than anything that had happened since. She wasn't talking to me in those brief moments of lucidity about her broken hip or the joys she'd experienced through her life, she was immersed in the pit of pressure and remorse for not learning how to forgive herself so that she could move forward. Who can imagine how she must have suffered.

And that's why it's crucial for us all to learn now so we don't waste any more of our precious energy. We need to let go of the need for accusations and guilt and make a wholesome route to forgive. There's nothing to be gained from going through life regretting an incident, failing to recognise a lesson or blaming someone else. It's completely fruitless and damages no one but ourselves.

"Never does the human soul appear so strong as when it forgoes revenge, and dares forgive an injury."
E H Chaplin

Latterly I've come to realise even more about forgiveness and the joy it can bring if we're prepared to be that honest. By allowing the unwillingness to forgive to become part of our makeup we're just making it another whipping stick, much like a character trait that's far out on the seesaw. It pulls us away from developing and hence hinders our progress up the spiral. Each of us has a journey to travel and a purpose to fulfil, and it's a remarkably easy way of avoiding doing so if we can blame someone else for causing a block in the road! This way we don't have to look to our own bad habits and characteristics as a way to better ourselves, we just have to remain focused on the block.

That's where the 'cop out' mentioned earlier is levied. It's not that we're letting other people off the hook for being disingenuous or discourteous towards us, it's that we can't be bothered or bear to face the truth about ourselves. Think about this.

In order to recognise that we're going the wrong way with our development we need to be completely honest. There's no swaying away from the centre line with this, I'm advocating an all-or-nothing approach. We can go in baby steps if you prefer but that would slow our progress and this is one aspect of self-development that needs our full attention.

To be able to forgive is the most powerful form of self-development that there is and it will take us furthest up the spiral. It's not about negating our feelings as if wiping them off a blackboard: it's about seeing them as part of the equation. By sifting through the knowledge we'll come to a quicker resolution and be able to free ourselves to forgive.

Let's look at another example.

Patrick has a need to be liked but deep down doesn't believe he's likeable. He goes out of his way to create similar scenarios so to remain in a repetitive cycle, providing a level of comfort as a result. As hard as this is for him to accept, he's prepared to listen.

In his school years he was a prefect. He took this to mean he was perfect simply because the words looked so similar. Being dyslexic he couldn't see the difference; they made a similar shape so to him they meant the same things.

What he didn't realise was the sense of power this gave him was formed by being so out of balance. He started to enjoy ordering other boys about, speaking down to them and generally became unpleasant. He used to set unimaginable tasks to make fun of some of the younger boys and lost respect from his peers in the process. Some of his closer friends drew away, not wanting to be associated with him, which hurt him and made him more determined to be 'powerful'.

He didn't have a very happy family life. His father was controlling and unpleasant, belittling Patrick's abilities, which contributed to the power struggle in his head when he became a prefect. His mother in contrast was 'fragile' and would spend hours at a time in bed, particularly when his father was home.

More recently Patrick has come to realise how shamefully he behaved through those school years and would like to turn the clock back. His personal growth has been stunted as a result due to the repetitive cycle he created. By not admitting to himself the part he played in becoming unpopular and not being able to see the bigger picture he's lived a life where, no matter how upsetting, he's recreated similar scenarios to remain in familiar territory.

Remorse is a force to be reckoned with. It's powerful in its own right but that doesn't always make it useful. Emotions are honest communications from our true self: if we're prepared to listen to them, they ensure that we extract the truth from a situation. Remorse, however, lies outside of this. It's like a pseudo-emotion that we hit ourselves over the head with time and again. It gains us no benefit.

Patrick's feelings of guilt, no matter how justified he considers them, get him absolutely nowhere. In fact they do quite the opposite as they ensure he remains very much entrenched in this pattern of thinking and behaviour that allow him no let-up. By replicating similar examples he's effectively ensuring that he's not likeable, to prove the point and punish himself in the process.

When we started to tease out the strands surrounding his feelings of loneliness and being unlikeable, it was this period in school, where he felt his friends had turned on him, his father was draconian and he hated himself, that bothered him the most. So this was where we began our therapy.

Forgiveness was at the heart of all of this. By not being able to forgive himself for his own behaviour, his friends for 'turning against him', and his father for being a bully, he perpetuated the re-establishments of these feelings through his life. Effectively, by holding on to the pain and blame, his hands were full, he left himself no other choice. However, if he put them down and moved away from this repetitive cycle he'd be able to bring fresh and invigorating experiences into his life.

To enable him to do this we worked through the varying layers of self-dismissal to give him a good overview. Then we looked at his characteristics and started to bring the weightier ones into balance. We looked at how his father's influence was less than nutritional, how replicating examples kept him very much stuck, and the counter-balance between his parents. He started to realise how he'd confused 'powerful' with becoming popular.

Once we'd done this he gained a far better perspective without self-judgement or remorse. Not only could he see the sense in forgiving but he started to 'put down' the feelings of guilt and hurt that he'd held onto for all these years and began to implement a more positive approach towards forgiveness.

We didn't try to push away the memories of his prefect days as if they were something disgusting or unlovable; we untangled them compassionately so that we could see the messages held within. This allowed him to gain some self-respect and love of himself and his parents. He started to see his father in a different light, realising the pressures he'd been under to *appear* as having a 'normal' family life when in fact his wife was always ill and his child had learning difficulties (which at that time were very misunderstood).

His father had died some months before our first session, so he couldn't reconcile the relationship but we evened out the imbalance which allowed Patrick to move further up the spiral and gain new learning and experiences as a result. The toughest part of all this was for Patrick to forgive himself and to drop all the accusations of self-hate and guilt that he'd perpetuated over years and learn to like himself.

And that's how you forgive. It's not by simply saying, 'I forgive you' as if a magical cure, you have to really *feel* it deep within. To say, 'I'm sorry, I forgive you' is a fabulous start and if, like the lady in the hospital, there's genuine remorse, it goes a long way to achieving it. But if we're not honest with our intentions it's not going to happen miraculously.

Honesty is at the heart of forgiveness as it is with all self-development, but to truly forgive requires the greatest depth of trust there is. We have to work at understanding and releasing the past so that we don't leave anything inside to fester. We need to appreciate how we contributed to an incident and how our characteristics become mirrored. We forgive others as a way of forgiving ourselves, but it's not always easy. We have to work through many layers in order to achieve this and, if we're not honest, we'll come back to the lesson again.

None of us are perfect; we all struggle to get things right at times and we've a wealth of learning to undertake. But if we accept that deep down we're all the same, we all share similar characteristics, once we've come more into alignment and reconnected universally at this level we'll blossom.

Exercise

Have you ever thought, 'I'll never forgive him/her?' If you have, this is a great place to start. If you haven't, think back to a moment where you've dismissed someone's feelings and felt guilty about it.

When an incident keeps coming back into our minds it's because we haven't taken all the learning from it. It could be because we haven't considered another person's actions as forgivable, or that ours were less then savoury. But the fact that we keep reconnecting with it means there's an aspect of it that still needs to be released. It's as if a little thread joins the two, reminding us to go back and extract all the learning we can from it.

Can you imagine what it would be like if there was a whole host of these experiences dragging along behind us? Think how tiring it would be, let alone how difficult negotiating the twists of the spiral would become, catching on each thorny leaf as we go by. It doesn't bear thinking about. But that's exactly what we should do if we want to release the weight of them. We don't want to remain tied to all these cameos of experiences as a way to prove a point or to claim that we've had the experience when all we're doing is refusing to learn the lesson.

So, with this in mind, we're going to release these threads that hold us to the experiences with love and care to the universe and allow them to flourish in an appropriate way to encourage growth within us.

Take the incident that you've identified and start to work through all the characteristics involved as a way to free yourself from the weight of them. Once you've done so expand this a little further by looking at how you've replicated similar experiences to provide a 'place of comfort'. Look at why forgiveness has been so hard for you. Has holding on to this pain or upset been of benefit or detriment? Are you trying to conform to another person's wishes by not forgiving rather than doing what's right for you?

Does this behaviour in any way contribute to the other person's lack of success or are you feeling resentful that they have gone on to enjoy their life? Work deeper through the layers, like peeling away an onion, until you've reached the real core.

Remember this is done from a place of detachment and with honesty; there is no sense of judgement. This way you'll get a much clearer understanding of all that's involved without reconnecting with the emotions of it.

When you're ready to forgive, let it go with love, there's nothing to hold on for. Once you've done so you will feel more positive and lighter, and memories that once tormented you will become stories you once heard somewhere. Truly a Life-Changing Moment!

Dwell on this

The love in our hearts is the fodder we live on

SECTION THREE

Section Three

Chapter 9 – The power of cleansing.

As we work through this book we're forming a community of spirit. We're attracting like-minded people who are equally motivated to gain a much brighter and more positive attitude of self.

This isn't about self-centredness and one-upmanship, or even self-focus to the exclusion of others. It's about *purity* of spirit, the unveiling of our truest of natures for everyone else.

This isn't the only reason for doing all this work, since we're primarily concerned with our own self-development, but it's a wonderful effect.

How we behave is of great concern to us. If we've muddied the waters in the past we'll struggle to project a pure enough image. It's a bit like looking through a dirty window, the grime that builds up on it over years will discolour our outlook. Likewise it will affect how others see us.

We need to find ways to clean this without allowing big-headedness to creep in. By keeping our own 'house' in order we're encouraging progress without wasting energy on past mistakes or lack of belief.

There are many stages to self-development and they all need to have a purpose, otherwise we'd be wasting our time. When it comes to cleansing – clearing away the effects of negative patterning - the same high ideal applies. We want to ensure our progress isn't tainted by negative experiences from our past or the people around us. Once we've reached a certain level we won't need to do this so often, but until then we need to reaffirm our position by cleansing every day.

Whatever the level of development we're looking at, it will reveal its relevant subjects. Cleansing is no different. However, we need to be specific on one point – **everything** that we allow to affect us negatively will act

as our nemesis and it will pull us away from the state of oneness to which we so aspire.

With continued effort and self-belief we can be as powerful as world leaders when it comes to changing things for the good, but we have to put our learning into practice if we're to make this happen.

To help us we'll use an image we can refer to whenever we're struggling with a distraction. It's not meant as a stand-alone method to put things right, as we'd need to work through the messages and levels incorporated within the experience for that, but, if we can see the ultimate effect, it will help us make the right choice.

Imagine there's a long straight path ahead and on either side are swathes of green silky grass being tickled by the warm summer breeze. This path runs along the top of the highest mountain ridge and as far as we can see in all directions are further mountainous ranges and deep troughs, the bottoms of which are out of our view.

Our path is open and inviting, there are no boulders to walk round or pebbles to slip on. Our view is totally un-obscured. Further along the path is a bench we can sit on and appreciate the view if we wish. There's no pressure to do so, it's totally up to us. We're surrounded by the purest sense of peace; there are no distractions or noise to interfere with this unadulterated state of bliss.

This is how we want our picture to look every time we check in on it.

Life's 'ups and downs' inevitable leave an imprint, drawing us away from the line we're walking, endangering our sense of self. The path may seem to narrow or become rocky, making it harder to navigate. The vegetation may alter, indicating a harsher environment, the weather could turn nasty or, worse still, the path could become completely obscured or impassable, making it impossible for us to progress.

And that's why we have this image, to help us identify the *effect* of the environment we are in. The people we associate with and the types of behaviour we exhibit will affect our overall sense of peace and wellbeing, which will reflect in the image of the path on top of the mountain.

Cleansing motivates us to gain and maintain a better view. It helps us discover aspects we weren't aware of before. By cleaning away the layers of 'grime' that have built up over the years we're not only becoming spiritually brighter, like a renaissance painting that has been restored to reveal the true depths of colour and fine detail, but we'll gain a better sense of self. It's like a bud opening after a long, harsh winter to reveal the most beautiful of flowers.

How we do this is twofold, since we need to be aware of cleansing our imprint on the ethereal levels, as well as our attitudes and behaviours closer to home. We've already discovered the importance of our characteristics in terms of their appearance and how they rebound onto others less suspecting of their effects when we're not in control, now we're going to accommodate the ethereal cleanse.

We're going to start with a very powerful visualisation that's been used for some years. It suits most people but, if it's not right for you, then decipher an equivalent. We call it 'The Sieve' and it's hugely beneficial if we use it every day as part of our cleansing ritual.

The Sieve

Stand with your feet slightly apart, distributing your weight evenly through both legs, feeling your centre of balance. Close your eyes and allow your breathing to steady into a slow rhythmic pattern allowing your arms to hang by your sides.

Imagine you're standing in a large garden sieve and on a long in-breath, mentally raise the sieve up through your body towards your neck. As it goes up it's collecting an array of unimaginable material that's accumulated. Don't worry about what this is, just allow it to happen.

The sieve may start to feel heavy or won't go past a certain point. That's fine, each time you use it it's going to behave slightly differently as it deciphers the level of cleansing that's required and acts accordingly. The more you do this, the better you'll be able to gauge the message it gives purely by gaining experience.

Once the sieve has reached the level of your throat, imagine your hands are grasping either side of it and, on an out-breath, mentally push it through and out of the top of your head. Hold it there whilst a brilliant white light vaporises the contents, dispelling all negativity to the ether.

Once the sieve is empty, bring it back down to settle beneath your feet, giving it a little twist in place ready for the next cleansing. You can bring the light down with it to dissolve any specks of negativity that may have remained, optimising its performance.

This is the basic cleansing I'd recommend doing every day. It's not time-consuming and makes a huge difference. However, you can take this a stage further by imagining that a lotus flower on the top of your head is opening up. As it does so the bright white light can stream in, filling you with its brilliance. Take it deeper with each in-breath until you feel completely filled.

Having done so, imagine the white light being pushed out of our physical self into an area just beyond. So with the next in-breath, bring more vitality and light within before pushing it out through your physical body *in*to the area just outside. It tends to be easier to imagine doing this on the out-breath.

This will provide a greater sense of protection and you'll generally feel more comforted and secure. Continue doing this until you feel completely nourished, providing a sense of padding around yourself. This is your inherent protection, known by many as your aura; we need to keep it 'puffed up' as much as possible and this is a wonderful way of doing so. If you feel your arms start to move ever so slightly away from your body whilst you're doing this, just allow it to happen. It's physical confirmation of what you're achieving.

When you've finished, close the lotus flower on the top of your head and give thanks for the assistance. You could go a stage further by asking for some guidance. It may come as an image or word 'dropping' into your head, a feeling or memory. However it comes, just be grateful and accept it. If you're not comfortable with this, that's fine, do so when you're ready. If you don't instantly sense the guidance, don't worry, it's a progressive exercise and, with perseverance and grace, will help you develop your intuition.

So how else can visualisations help us?

Baths and showers are great places to create cleansing visualisations. They provide the right environment to cleanse both our etheric and physical body at the same time, washing away the day's grime.

When in the shower, imagine the water has a secret ingredient - a magical formula that purifies and cleans. The grime that's accumulated on our etheric body over the day, weeks or even years can be seen very differently, depending on our own visualisation skills. If we allow our minds to rove for a moment, we'll see it for ourselves. It can look slimy and suffocating, or caked on like dry mud. It could be all over us, or just the odd smudge here and there. Don't be put off by how it presents, it will look different to each person and at different times. Just relax and let your intuition work for you.

Once we've seen the grime that's settled on us, we need to dissolve its effect. The water, as we've discovered, holds these magical qualities. It loosens the very 'dirt' that we've mentioned so that it can wash it away. The power of imagery is very important here as the stronger we can visualise, the more powerfully it will work. Make sure you wash every part of you in this way, we don't want to leave anywhere un-cleansed!

Try holding the shower head in your hand and use it like a jet wash. It's immensely satisfying to see it being blasted off.

Likewise, when in a bath, mentally allow the grime to dissolve into the water. Or better still, imagine it being 'pulled' off you like a snake shedding skin as you lie in the bath whilst the water drains away.

There are numerous other visualisations that are just as effective. Play around with ideas. Some people use different coloured water to dispel negativity; others like to towel themselves roughly to ensure every bit is removed, buffing their body in the process. There's no right or wrong way to do this: so long as it gives the effect of being cleansed, that's all we're concerned about.

It can be beneficial to cleanse before going to bed as a way of dispelling negative thoughts before we sleep. Likewise, in the morning it can be invigorating and start us off on the right foot. Just so long as we incorporate it into our da, at some point it will do us good.

How we achieve a level of cleansing is up to personal choice but now we need to understand what this 'grime' is in the first place so we can stop attracting it to ourselves.

"Better keep yourself clean and bright. You are the window through which you must see the world."

George Bernard Shaw

Feeling 'yucky' or 'out of sorts' is a common enough complaint but do we ever stop to think what it really indicates? Our innate sense of self is trying to tell us that something isn't quite right, that we need to adjust things or take notice. Often, the cleansing methods we've just discussed will be enough to ease this sense of disgruntlement, or at least go some way towards it. But if we want to really progress then we need to uproot the negative cycles responsible for creating such feelings of lethargy or unrest contributing to our sense of being off-colour.

When I've mentioned self-doubt or lack of confidence, it's not by way of being defamatory: it's to encourage self-belief. To work on ourselves in the way we've already started to is character-forming and confirms our true nature; it provides us with far more information about who we are and how we interact with other people than we realise. Not only does this help us to identify our own characteristics and the remodelling of them, but also to understand how other people respond to us.

When we interact with other people we do so on a subliminal level as well as on a physical and emotional level. This may be obvious for those more spiritually aware, but for the majority, who are less likely to appreciate this subliminal activity, they will go about their day in total ignorance of the fact that negativity imprints carcinogenically on them. It eats away at the heart of them creating dis-ease and disgruntlement.

When we talk about attracting 'grime' to us in this way, it's this level of inflection that we are discussing. We're not looking for someone or something to blame for our inability to be 'refreshing,' but we are interacting on the subliminal level where sense and reason are not considered. If we want to understand something at 'face value,' the spoken word is a perfect example: it's clear and succinct and we all understand what's happening. However, if we're to ascertain the response to this, then it's to the subliminal levels that we need to look in order to see the real effect.

Let me explain a bit further. We damage ourselves with how much we're prepared to accept from other people in order to try and keep them happy. I'm not talking about jobs or responsibilities as a way to help them out, although this can become overpowering; I'm talking about the subliminal transference of information that's not so good for us.

What they lay on us in terms of 'grudge' (grime and sludge) on our metaphoric window, the subliminal transference of information we've just spoken about, comes from their less endearing aspects - their least-balanced characteristics that leave them somewhat out on the extremities of the seesaw. This is the information they relay to us and campaign to smear us with to make themselves feel more worthy, thereby lessening our ability to see out clearly or been seen for our true natures. It's rather as if we've been smeared by a slug trail or have been used as a doormat to clean their feet on without realising we're allowing it. This distraction directs our attention away from their actual behaviour and focuses on the effects.

Once our windows are obscured we're less able to see out objectively and so our sense of reasoning narrows. This leaves us with either the instinct to attack (usually verbally) as a form of defence, or to shrink back into a corner and wait it out until things improve. Neither option is acceptable as both leave us 'not in control.' We're not being responsible for our own efforts or short failings. We're being moulded on someone else's behaviour rather than remaining true to ourselves, which is the opposite of what we are trying to achieve with our spiritual progression.

If we imagine we're in a space that's poorly lit, we could get the sense that the walls are closing in on us purely because we can't see the room properly. Likewise, our heads could run away with unimaginable scenarios because we've become fearful. If we don't have the correct information to make sound judgements and we don't know what's lurking in the shadows we could start to feel out of our comfort zone. This could cause us to experience feelings of worry or panic purely because we haven't remained within what we know is honest and true, our emotional communicators. By shooting up to our heads to work things out rather than remaining more centred around our heart level we've lost the benefit of the equilibrium gained, so lost 'sight' of the reality of the situation. This could result in the loss of the lovely relaxed, secure feeling we've previously had and the ability to react appropriately all because we need to switch the light on!

And this is what is happening when we're with certain people. They narrow our sense of vision by dirtying our metaphoric window to such an extent that we can't see out objectively. We're trapped in the corners of the darkened room waiting for the light to be switched on. But we can't allow this indication of loss of self to happen as we're already aware of so much. By seeing and being seen through them, essentially we're becoming a reflection of them. Even if it's from the opposite perspective, their behaviour, as much as we don't condone it, is being confirmed as acceptable because we're allowing ourselves to be pushed to the other end of the seesaw to balance with them. From this we can see how disastrous this could be if we don't 'lighten up' from their weightiness by ritually cleansing until we become more aware of how people imprint on us negatively and find a way to stop it from happening.

Much like placing a tint over a camera lens, it will affect the colour of every photograph taken. We're recognising the effects of this smeared grime on our metaphoric window by our feelings and behaviour. We're concerned with what's happening on a subliminal level, and that's why our cleansing routine is so important. If we don't clean this grime off regularly, it will build up and make us porous, thereby absorbing less appealing characteristics which will result in feelings of 'yucky' and 'out of sorts.'

There's always a balance in everything we do and so, in contrast, if we associate with like-minded people we'll be improving our subliminal connection. We'll be associating with finer and purer aspects simply because we're developing and so won't be smearing each other's metaphoric windows.

Often we draw needier people to us because subliminally they want to be a reflection of us. Much like a moth to the light, they are attracted to our energy. They feed on us as a way to feel better about themselves, sucking some of our energy in the process. As much as this doesn't sound spiritual, it's a fact and one we need to address.

Daily cleansing will help with this to an extent, as it will provide a level of distance from them. But, if we want to be more effective we need to be honest with who we spend time with, where we go and how we think. It's a continual cycle of living purposefully, where our attitudes and characteristics are being constantly brought into check, reflecting our real sense of being rather than just letting things happen. It's no wonder some mystics have escaped 'normal' life preferring to spend it up the side of a mountain away from all of this!

And that's where our image can help. If we walk the straight and narrow (along the top of our mountain) and are aware of the pitfalls (the steep slopes and boulders) we can stay more true to our natures. We'll reflect the goodness that's within, without taking on the extremes of other people's characteristics in the process. When we come unstuck and feel disillusioned or out of sorts, we can refer back to our path to see the point we have reached and what the image informs us without any sense of self-judgement. It won't provide an instant fix, but it'll give us a good insight into the problem and help as to how to move forward.

Exercise

Cleanse every day. Decide how you're going to do it. I suggest you use the sieve and add additional methods such as the bath or shower if you want to. Mentally cleanse your home, your car, your office; cleanse your children, your husband or wife. Some people find sage very useful for cleansing rooms. There are various crystals that can be useful as well, start to research them. Surround yourself only with possessions that are uplifting. If you find that a picture is dark or depressing, move it somewhere less conspicuous or get rid of it. Tune into everything in your house to feel if its energy is good. If it isn't, let it go.

Don't hold onto to past relationships by way of possessions. If you feel that by keeping an item you are somehow still connected with that person, be honest about why you would want to do this. Some relationships sour and so it's a good way to be free of them by removing every item connected with that person from your house. Having a bonfire can be cathartic as it cleanses subliminally whilst removing the physical presence, or have a car boot sale and give the money raised to a charity. There are numerous ways you can do this without appearing spiteful or aggrieved.

Release with love and let your past friends be free to learn their lessons whilst you go up your spiral of success. By not letting go you are the only one being damaged by stirring up memories best left to rest.

Clear out clutter, it's a breeding ground for negative energy. Make your bedroom fresh and clean. Avoid dark colours, lighten up!

Look at what you read and watch on T.V. Is it compatible with your new resolve to be spiritual? How do you feel having watched a soap or thriller? Happy and uplifted or tense and grim? Become aware of everything you do and see. This is a lifelong commitment, not just for one week.

Dwell on this

The first step to recognition is to realise what stops it.

Section Three

Chapter 10 – Dreaming

Dreams are a source of fascination to me. Not only because they show how extraordinary we are but because they contain information way above our usual levels of comprehension. To think we can transcend life whilst asleep is quite incredible.

Dreams have often been explained as a way of sifting through life experiences, fulfilling the role of paper shredder and informant. But, as important as that is, it's the far deeper level of spiritual prowess that we're going to look at.

Dreams are as much a part of us as talking, walking and eating, but we're often so busy with our everyday lives that we overlook the importance of them. It's not that we don't dream, as some would profess, it's that we don't always remember them. Our ability to forget is due to the levels of our purity being challenged; we're happily filling our lives with dramas and upset, unaware of the real consequence.

And that's where our spiritual health becomes compromised. We're effectively blocked from receiving information from our 'higher selves' because we're not considered a reliable enough conduit. As painful as this is for us to accept, we need to appreciate this fact and start to correct it. Otherwise we'll remain on the more superficial layers where desensitisation and dramas are commonplace and we'll forego the pleasures of connecting with wisdom and grace when asleep.

We've caused a block by being too 'gross,' but if we turn this about we'll be able to connect more easily. It's all about effort. In order to achieve this we need to ensure our sense of purpose isn't smeared with the effects of lower vibrational activity, the forms of entertainment considered less than savoury when relaxing. We're not talking about dinners with friends or playing a musical instrument, but the more fundamental aspects of 'entertainment', when watching television, lurid activity or drinking amounts of alcohol are rife. The higher we progress up the spiral the faster our vibrational rate becomes, it's an effect that confirms we're heading towards a crystalline form where purity is the entrance. If we transgress these layers with lower vibrational activity we're in effect turning our backs on our target, slipping away from the pinnacle of success.

Our dreams don't just contain spiritual lessons and advice, they involve us in the world outside ourselves where consciousness meets the dynamics of the universe. It's a little like spiritual sleepwalking, only better, as we actually remember the effects in our subconscious.

If we consider dreams are just a part of this then we're gaining a better insight into the potential. We're not talking about dynamism purely in terms of force, we're addressing a uniqueness far outside of this, where full exposure would ensure us harm. This is partly why our route becomes blocked; if we're not prepared for it and haven't the level of purity required we won't be able to accommodate the wisdom we 'pull' through, thereby risking harm to ourselves and the potential pollution of the levels we've been accessing. It's a two-way street where information is passed freely between us. It's only our lack of ability to meet the necessary criteria that blocks the flow.

So what are these dreams meant to convey, now we're beyond thinking of them as random matter and ramblings of the subconscious?

Dreams appear as snapshots of movie clips and flashes of images, before progressing into knowledge. The more we connect with this, the more we can build on the wisdom and reflect it outwardly to all we meet.

When we've learnt how to develop our levels of purity, we'll be able to increase this connection whilst asleep and gain a more detailed understanding of 'life.' This will ensure the information is passed freely and is of better quality whilst at the same time we'll be enhancing our skills as a better conduit. Until then we're blocking a source of enormously useful information by failing to reach the levels of purity required.

As important as it is to be open and receptive during this process, we need to have the courage to release any fears that surround us when working at these higher levels, as this alone is enough to create a block. We're not dabbling in black magic or doing anything unscrupulous, so there's nothing to worry about, it's a purely natural phenomenon that enhances our true identity. Any resistance is more likely to come from our own attitude towards growth rather than anything more concerning, and if this is the case we can always look at this.

When we're ready to cross the barrier into the higher realms, we'll do so expertly. There's nothing to do except enjoy the experience because we'll have done all the work beforehand. If you're feeling sceptical at this stage, why not give it a go and see for yourself?

Gaining access, albeit for limited periods, provides us with rapid growth. We're not concerned with how we got there, just how to make the best use of it. If we're worried we may not have enough courage or experience, put these concerns aside as we all have what it takes, and there's no prize for intelligence. But if you've tried to access these heights in the day without success, why not try it this way at night?

Our intuition helps us manage the connection between dreams and spiritual prowess beautifully - we just need to let it happen. By letting ourselves go rather than trying to control the outcome, we're giving ourselves the best opportunity to develop. And that's what we're doing with this book, developing our opportunity for growth.

Over the years we've been conditioned to ignore our natural rhythms in preference to serving our thoughts. Now we're moving into a new era where our focus is all important. We're not concerned with what others may think but with the ability to progress supernaturally, to achieve oneness with the greatest power that there is.

Before going to bed we need to encourage an environment that's conducive to spiritual growth. It's fantastic to think we can nurture this when asleep but we repair functionally on one level as we develop on another.

Our dreams become our whispering thoughts, they guide us when we least expect. We're all aware of them to some degree but, if we're distracted by dramas and unsavoury characteristics, we're not giving them a fair enough chance and so lose the benefit as a result. They are our foremost link with our higher selves. They provide a way through the layers of spirituality until we reach the level appropriate to us at that time. We're not able to pick the route - it's a progressive procedure that's very much dependent on our position on the spiral. But if we want to make this work, then it's our level of spirituality here on earth that will make the difference.

The layers provide a form of protection, not for us, but for the higher realms. Much of what happens on earth is considered far too coarse to pass through the varying filters, and so we get stuck. But if we want to benefit from the lessons, we need to make the effort to reduce the 'coarseness' around us so that we can pass through some of the filters and gain knowledge.

Dreams instigate change, develop a sense of purpose or a life-enhancing skill amongst many other benefits. If we're not prepared to develop, then we're turning our backs on a wonderful tool. This doesn't mean we won't dream but we won't reach the level of maturity that's possible because we're too gross. We'll become stuck somewhere between our hopes and expectations of self and our full potential.

And that's why this is so important: if we don't take our preparations before sleep seriously, we're not making the best use of the opportunity.

"Cherish your visions and your dreams as they are the children of your soul, the blueprint of your ultimate achievements."

Napoleon Hill

Our thoughts distract us from our true sense of self. They pull us away from the point of oneness we've so often mentioned through this book and steer us towards repetitive cycles. If we want to change this then one way we can do so is by looking at how we fill our heads in the hours before bed. It would be even better if we could incorporate the whole day but to isolate this period is a good start.

These times are so very precious to us because they often contain the time we spend with our families and friends, as well as being the preparation time for our 'travels.'

When we're asleep we're blending with angelic presence, gaining access to wisdom and grace way above our normal ability. But if we restrict ourselves with anxieties or superstition we're essentially forming another way to hold ourselves back, turning ourselves into a shadow of other people's insecurities.

So why do we need this connection at night?

There's so much more to us than the physical self, but it can be challenging to believe so. As a result we rely on our heads to work things out rather than trust our intuition. As we progress we'll see the benefit of stepping away from this rigid conditioning and combine both methods to provide answers.

If we spend hours a day watching television, for example, we're filling our heads with content that confirms we live in a fearful place where extremes of characters, violence and desensitising material are a part of us purely because it's in the programmes. I don't say we're going to start rushing around being crazed mass-murderers or the like, but we will become desensitised as a result.

If we want to progress then we need to recognise the importance of this and stop watching this type of stuff. Our will to succeed needs to be stronger than the lure to such material. After all, we don't want to risk clogging our abilities to be receptive just because we're spiritually incapable of recognising this.

And that's the controversy we're left with. Do we feed our lesser desires for drama and sensationalism, gossip and histrionics, or adhere to our truer nature of being spiritually selective?

This isn't a decision anyone can make for us, we're each responsible for our own progression. But if we're serious about moving up the spiral then we need to look at this level of infection.

If we take the period from 6pm until bed, it's enough time to make a difference without it becoming too arduous. Everything during that time needs to be done purposefully so as not to clog up the filters, resulting in a negative response. Often these are the hardest hours of the day to be purposeful, as tiredness has an effect, so if we can master this period it should be that much easier to incorporate the rest of the day at some point. If we're not ready to forego watching television then that's OK: just as long as we're prepared to accept the limitation this brings, we can always come back to it later on.

Once we've refrained from this kind of activity for a month or more we'll see the sense in changing. We'll feel more centred and upbeat, having lost the draw to that form of entertainment. We'll wonder how we ever managed to find time to watch so much 'telly' as our lives become filled with rewarding experiences. We may even have learnt a new skill or hobby in the process!

What we read comes in to this as well, so don't swap one method of distraction for another! If we're serious about progressing we need to stop pulling up the drawbridge to accessing wisdom in this way and start to benefit from the experience.

When we've had a few weeks of purposeful evenings we'll discover our dreams become purposeful as well. They'll enrich our lives to such an extent that we won't want to go back to the old ways. We'll adjust to this new level of learning and blossom as a result.

We won't be saying our behaviour doesn't matter, as if ignorant. Instead we'll become responsible; we'll be working at a level far higher than we're used to, where extremes of character and drama-seeking thrills are less attractive, thus helping to form a more universally-connected society.

But this won't happen until we're ready to sustain our role. We're enhancing our ability to grow and by keeping a more positive attitude we'll be able to eradicate much of the darkness that surrounds us. But, if we're continually bombarded with less than savoury examples through what we watch, we'll lose much of the benefit.

At times 'grossness' appears when we least expect it. Whether it's because a television programme has turned unexpectedly, or an argument ensued with a loved one, we're not immune from its proximity. But if we can distance ourselves, acknowledge what's happening and the lessons involved, we'll be putting ourselves back on track with the minimum of fuss.

The more complicated our lives become, the more 'normal' the extremes of behaviour will seem. This is because we become so overstretched that it's impossible to keep all the angles covered. It's like our radar becomes out of kilter, which is of great concern as if we don't have our antennae in full working order we're not going to sense what's right for us. Our resolve gets weakened, which increases our acceptance, bringing us more of the same. We even start to mimic the behaviour as if it's normal and acceptable.

In order to break this cycle we need to live more purposefully and be aware of every decision we make so that we can work our way up the spiral.

If we try and eradicate the 'grossness' from our lives between the hours of 6pm and bed, we're going a long way towards this. But we need to fill this space with something more nutritional so that we are not creating a void that other people can 'leak' into, as instinctively they'll feel nourished by the energy and try to take it for themselves. We've created this wonderful space to flourish in, so we don't need others less willing to make the effort trying to absorb it.

Eating health foods, being playful or relaxing with music is a great start. Avoid the television and computer but use the time to interact with family or friends, learn a new skill — something creative, this always opens up new pathways, or go for a walk. Do an exercise class, read an inspiring book or meditate. Just so long as we're at peace and don't let anything during this time interfere with the purpose of raising our vibrations, we'll keep *clear* enough to converse through the night.

Having done so, we'll see the sense in it. We'll feel more relaxed and interested. We won't switch off the minute the television gets turned on, but we'll start to use our senses to develop. We'll feel the 'weight' from old forms of entertainments dissolve, and won't want them back again. Our nights will improve, not only in the context already mentioned but in the quality of sleep. Rather than turning to medication to promote rest, maybe this could help!

Exercise

Take a single programme that you've watched for a while that either contains a lot of violence, histrionics, glorification of negative behaviours or anything else that's not in line with our spiritual approach, and stop watching it.

Fill this time instead with something far more nutritional. Maybe use the times it was on to work on balancing a trait or starting a new interest. Do this for several weeks until the sense of 'wanting' to see that programme wanes.

Having had a break from it for several weeks, go back and watch just one episode. Monitor how it makes you feel. Do you feel dirty, tense, heavy or lacklustre? Or maybe just not so happy? This is wonderful confirmation that what we call entertainment isn't always so amusing.

It's also beneficial to make a chart of exactly how many hours of television you watch in a week, so that you can monitor your progress. It may just be the odd night, which is less significant, but for many it's continuously until they go to bed. If you could choose just one thing that would make your life feel more fulfilled, what would it be? How could these new-found free hours be used to achieve this?

If we continually block our route to superlative advice we're going to slow our progress.

Unlike working on our traits, here we're changing a habit, so it's going to be more difficult. It won't go unnoticed that we've altered how we spend our evenings, so we need to be sure why we're doing it. By changing our behaviours we're showing ourselves as fully committed.

Solitude comes into this as it confirms a level of comfort with ourselves. We're often so caught up with the noise and frenetic pace of the world that it almost seems frightening to be without it. But we're *choosing* to step away from the continual bombardment to allow a sense of peace to appear. Don't be fooled into thinking we're just substituting one form of 'distraction' for another, the noise in exchange for feelings of isolation. This is illusory and holds no substance. So long as we respect ourselves and the time we devote to it, we'll never regret the space we've found.

Our goal is to raise our vibrations, which give us our sense of purpose. We won't find peace in a kitchen full of people, or the lounge with pop music blaring. We need to find quiet time away from the continual sensory overload of modern living and just *be*. By taking this time in the evenings we're making the right choice for ourselves. We're not being led into brain-numbing activities for the purpose of conforming but instead we're finding time for quiet contemplation, where we can get back in touch with ourselves, develop our intuitions and lose any fear of being alone.

Our dreams will become more meaningful as we start to remember them. They may even offer wisdom and guidance for the months ahead. Don't worry about this, we're championing the effects of spiritual development and it's fantastic! We're becoming spiritually mature, standing with a foot either side of the fulcrum of our seesaw, making a link between heaven and earth.

The more we do this, the higher the perspective from which we'll see. We'll become less judgemental and insecure and won't need to be the centre of attention. We're not interested in the dumbing experiences that kept us 'stuck' in the past, we're content with who we are.

And that's important. We're no longer searching for ourselves as if continually lost, we've found someone we can believe in. We're spiritually awakened and experience love and forgiveness in equal measures. There's no need for self-judgement which stunts our growth and we're more accepting of mistakes whether they be our own or someone else's.

I'm not saying interaction with our family and friends is now less necessary, as of course it's hugely important. But the balance between love and support, friendship and self-development needs to be considered. If we think about what we do, who we spend our time with and how this affects our sense of self, we'll go a long way to ensuring this progress.

If we find ourselves in less-than-wholesome situations, we must take notice of the effect. How can this experience gain us further learning? We can protect ourselves to a certain extent by putting up a mental barrier to any negativity by imagining ourselves dressed in suits of armour or standing behind a mirror, thereby preventing it from penetrating our developing sensitivities. It would be kind if we could tilt the mirror away slightly so as to not 'fire' it straight back at them.

But if we really want to avoid the influence, we need to elude the situations in the first place. By reducing the time spent talking about dramas and gossiping we're effectively moving up the spiral. It encourages the wisdom of faith to flow through us, giving a *knowing* rather than a need to work things out. We're connecting with our higher selves more readily and gaining wisdom as a result. But this can't happen if we remain fascinated by the lower energies. We need to make a choice and stand by it if we want to reach our pinnacle of success.

This doesn't make us boring; on the contrary it gives us the freedom to be expressive, joyful and illuminating. It draws people to us rather than repels them. We'll also attract less well-developed people who want to ride piggy back, so be aware of this. It's not for us to carry anyone else and it won't help them in the long run if we did. Share wisdom and grace, but don't carry them, no matter how much it hurts not to do so. They have their lessons to learn and if we try to do it for them they'll have to begin their rotation on the spiral again.

By attracting people spiritually, we're asking to be accepted: we're willing to give and receive on an equal basis. If there isn't this mutual attraction, ask what the purpose is. Could it be a life lesson for you both or is someone looking for a hop up the spiral?

By connecting with the energies at night through the manner we've discussed, we're putting out a request for further wisdom and grace. We're achieving a level of learning that's so much easier to gain than having to experience it personally. We don't need to question how or why it's given, just so long as we are able to appreciate it.

Exercise

By applying the suggestion of preparing for sleep from 6pm, we're giving ourselves the best chance for this progression. So turn off the television, computers and loud music from then and make a point of being calm and peaceful. If you tend to take calls through the evening, try and restrict them. Maybe even turn the phones off after 8pm, so that you can be free from external distractions.

Prepare a freshly-cooked meal. Take your time over eating it and, if you live with friends or family, make it special time to be together. If you're eating alone, make it a time for reflection and quiet contemplation. Don't allow things that have happened through the day to keep replaying in your mind. Learn the lesson and let them go - it's not beneficial to hold on to the energy connected with them.

Imagine you're releasing the valve on a pressure cooker and allow the events of the day to escape slowly. If you're not comfortable with this imagery, make a list of all the aspects that are bothering you so you can get them out of your head.

Consider how your studies towards spiritual development have been reflected through incidents in the day. Without any sense of judgement and with detachment, allow yourself to dwell on the lessons to ensure they are learnt. There may have been a compliment or some praise you didn't accept as well as you could, or an antagonistic environment that could have been handled differently. Whatever the experience, congratulate yourself for recognising it, even if it is retrospectively. Remember there's no sense of self-judgement, we're all learning and so need to treat each other and ourselves with respect.

Once you've done so, do something mindless. By this I mean nothing too taxing for the brain. Read an uplifting book, listen to classical music, play an instrument, do some knitting … relax. Let the day's worries go as you prepare to meet with your higher self during the night. Have a relaxing bath, talk about optimistic and exciting plans for the future with your family and friends, organise holidays or days out away from the normal pace of life.

Don't regurgitate painful memories for the sake of it or entertain negative discussions – this will shatter the illusion of pureness you've been creating. This is your time to be free from the influence of lower entities, so respect it.

When you go to bed, be receptive. Make your last thoughts as you 'drop off' peaceful and gracious. Give thanks for your day, for your children, your wife or husband. Send love to people you know, mentally ask them to forgive you if you feel it's necessary. Send healing love to people you know are unwell or in emotional turmoil.

Have a notebook beside your bed so, should you wake, you can jot down a dream before you forget it. Get into the habit of doing this on waking as it will be a marvellous reminder of wisdom that you've brought through. The more you do this, the more you'll remember until you'll be writing pages a day! Refer back to it regularly, as you'll see it contains much knowledge.

Try and hold onto the feelings of peace and space gained through the evening and night into the next day. This will help develop the sense of solitude and mindfulness that's so encouraged. It gains a level of detachment so that wisdom can flow through unimpeded, making your day that much more productive.

Don't let your head be a whirl of business worries all evening in the hope of solving them, or mull over arguments and upsets for hours. Allow your higher self to sort these out. By sleeping on them, having gone to bed in this purposeful state, you'll give yourself the best chance of gaining the correct result without having to suffer the upset. Trust yourself and know you'll always have the answers if you ask for them. Be patient and receptive as you await the reply.

If you're upset over some wrong-doing or filling your head with dramas and desensitising material, you're effectively blocking the receptivity you desire.

If you've a difficult letter or email to write, draft it but leave it until the next day before you send it. Be sure that it feels right to you when you reread it before sending. So often 'pearls of wisdom' are implanted through the night. Don't let your head make all the decisions; feel it from your heart, it will be much more honest. When you read it through again the next day, if it seems too abrupt or accusatory, you'll have the chance to amend it without having regrets for not handling it so well.

Dwell on this

When our thoughts are primarily about being a victim, we're at a stage that can get us furthermost up the spiral.

Section Three

Chapter 11 – nutrition

Now that we're applying cleansing to our daily lives, we're going to look at how maintaining a healthy lifestyle can increase the heights we achieve. When we talk of height it's not in the literal sense, of course: we're increasing our vibrations to gain further clarity, confidence and trust in who we are.

One way we can do this is through what we eat. Health and diet, like diet and self-development, go hand in hand, they're inseparable. In this chapter we're going to discover how we can use food to improve on the level we reach.

What we eat can have a profound effect upon the way we develop. Nutrition plays a vitally important part in all aspects of our development, but here we're going to consider the *energetic* effect.

If we eat in fast-food restaurants and consume microwave meals, we're not doing the best for ourselves. I'm not saying this to be controversial, as we all enjoy them from time to time, but if we continue to do so, we'll effectively hold ourselves back.

What we eat fuels our intention as much as our levels of purity, there's no getting away from this. If we use the analogy of putting fuel in our car we'll understand how crucial this is. We wouldn't put diesel in a petrol engine or let the tanks overfill or run too low. We're finely-attuned vehicles and as such need to respect this.

If we cram our bodies with less than wholesome ingredients, we're making it harder for ourselves. We're eating to improve ourselves now, not merely to fill a gap, so need to appreciate the difference. After just a few healthier meals we'll feel the benefit. But if the food doesn't sustain our energetic requirements, we'll lose the chance of raising our vibrations in this way, relying more heavily on other methods to achieve it. That's fine, there are other options, but why wouldn't we want to gain the maximum benefit for both our physical and spiritual wellbeing?

For the most part it's the lack of effort that holds us back, we drift back into old habits. More often than not we attribute this to cost, perceived or actual, without having the figures to back it up. But if we discovered that we could eat more healthily on a lower budget, would that make a difference?

By being selective we can save ourselves money *and* improve our health and levels of purity, how much better can it get? If we want to improve ourselves we need to address it from every angle. We're multi-faceted individuals and as such have to be prepared to look at many different avenues to get results. If we need confirmation of this, we need only look at people who are less aware and see how their eating habits and attitudes reflect their situation.

If we make widespread changes it'll be harder to maintain them, so we'll look at a few key areas to get us started and slowly expand on them.

Water is our number one focus. We're largely made of it and yet we often forget this. We drink when we're thirsty or out with friends, but don't seem to remember to keep ourselves hydrated at other times. If we allow our habits to overrule our sense of purpose, we'll fail to get past this point. We've already proved we're worthy of the investment, so now we need to follow through by making the effort.

When we wake it's the perfect opportunity to start the day with good intentions by drinking a glass or two or water. Rehydrating after sleep is very important as we lose water through breathing and sweating during the night. If you don't believe this test it for yourself, weigh yourself before you go to bed and when you first get up. There can be a noticeable difference, particularly when it's hot, so we need to compensate for this.

Water purifies and helps the body to eliminate waste from cellular activity. It also contributes to correct functioning of all our bodily systems. If we neglect this fact, we could potentially be harming ourselves. The single most important aspect to taking care of ourselves is to monitor our water intake, thereby providing the best environment for good health.

Another wonderful attribute to keeping hydrated is the ability to vibrate faster. It may seem of less importance but I stress it's not. If we want to develop, the primary consideration has to be the rate at which we vibrate. The higher we progress up the spiral, the greater our level of purity and hence our vibrational rate. This is reflected in everything we do. If we 'physically' remove the chance to resonate at this level through lack of water, we're limiting ourselves. By watching our fluid intake we can ensure our rate doesn't dip.

There's no need for costly equipment or purchases, and it's readily available. If we're concerned about additives then we can filter it but there's no need to buy expensive bottles from a supermarket if you don't wish to, that's down to personal choice.

For optimal function we need to eliminate the risk of dehydration so that we can vibrate at the level required. It aids our digestion, reducing the chance of constipation and disease. If we feel sluggish, more often than not it's as a result of lack of water, and it's an easy one to correct. On a more spiritual note constipation, like all disease, is an indication of what needs to happen. It can imply a blocked path, character traits that need to be looked at, such as lethargy and stubbornness, or a general lack of energy (movement) caused by losing sight of who we are or our sense of purpose, even becoming lazy as a result.

One of the key aspects of self-developing is to keep ourselves moving so the energy flows in the direction we would like. Like a turbine, if we allow ourselves to stop it takes more effort to get started again than it did to just maintain it.

We need to sustain the level of effort required to remain on top of our highest potential. We're not judging ourselves, we're adjusting to a new way of being, and it takes practice. If we're being harsh on ourselves we need to ask why. Would we be so unkind to someone else? When we slip back, as will inevitably happen at times, it's not the fact that we did so that should concern us, but understanding the lessons behind it. It's just a little bump in the road that we need to navigate with the minimum of fuss and re-establish the position of trust we had in ourselves.

"The doctor of the future will no longer treat the human frame with drugs, but rather will cure and prevent disease with nutrition."

Thomas Edison

When we talk about changing our diet, we're not demanding strict regimes that keep us focused on the more negative aspects of weight gain or weight loss, thereby setting us up with a challenge before we even start: we're going to approach this more gently in order to bring balance naturally. If it doesn't feel right, isn't a joy to incorporate and doesn't serve a higher purpose, then it's not spiritually attuned to our way of thinking.

If our diet consists mainly of processed meals, and contains additives and preservatives and lower vibrational foods such as processed bread, meat and non-organically-grown vegetables we're not giving ourselves the best opportunity to grow. We need to keep our metaphoric window clean without smearing it with lower vibrational activity. A way we can do this is by addressing our attitude towards growth and food, since they are indistinguishable. If we're focused on eating out of habit rather than what and when we need to, we'll always have the sense that we're being governed rather than being in control. By eating the amount to suffice, rather than maintaining the indoctrination of clearing our plates, we're being challenged. So many of our attitudes are developed from our childhoods and were probably applicable back then. But now we need to recognise them as a guiding arm rather than a prescription and adapt them for our own use. By being proactive in our approach we're taking responsibility for who we are, not making decisions based on advertising, childhood conditioning or other people's opinions.

If we incorporate some salads, organic vegetables, juices and raw food in our diet, we'll automatically feel less sluggish. We'll become more spiritually mature through what we eat, helping us feel more upright and centred, moving us closer to the fulcrum of our seesaw.

The thought of changing our diet can make some people feel quite anxious though, as often our existing diet ensures a level of comfort whilst masking deeper concerns. The more we lack courage and self-belief, the more we'll identify with this and our attitude towards food becomes less healthy. If we're not able to be honest in our approach, we may tend to brush over this chapter, discarding it as of little relevance. But it's just that sort of attitude that has led to worldwide problems, where poor diets and gluttony have contributed to health issues simply because we don't recognise the importance of nutrition, and here in the West we seem to be leading in this respect.

Causes of death are related to lifestyle – the genes load the gun but our lifestyle pulls the trigger. In the UK, heart disease is the number one killer, followed by respiratory disease, strokes, cancers and liver disease. Fifty years ago it was tuberculosis and pneumonia. In such a short span of time we have completely turned our medical history around, and in some ways are none the better for it.

Vitamin D deficiency is more recognised in high latitude countries where sunlight is more restricted, but coupled with the layering-on of sun blocks to protect from skin cancers without gaining the benefit. Much like everything we talk of in this book, it's the balanced approach we need to take.

Keeping our colons happy is imperative. Taking enough fibre in our diet is a must if we want to ensure smooth working to prevent disease. But most of us lack the motivation to maintain this, more often than not eating less than half of the daily recommended amount. If we eat something carcinogenic, our body's effort to eliminate it becomes hampered by slow progress, thereby allowing disease a window. Live yogurt and probiotic help with this alongside increasing our fibre intake. All plant-based foods contain fibre, some more than others, but meat, fish and dairy products don't contain any.

If we aren't prepared to adjust our diets, or the quantities we eat, we'll be prone to spiritual starvation. Whether we over or under-eat it's a form of compensation or punishment to ease the discomfort we feel. The fear is real and needs to be handled compassionately. If we start to dictate, making well-meaning alterations to someone else's diet we're as much responsible for any anxiety it may bring as the person who's masking the issues. As soon as they are aware of the problem within themselves then they can start to address the concerns, easing off the need for this crutch without feeling pressurised to do so.

I don't suggest that we make sweeping changes to our diet at this stage but that we slowly eliminate the least beneficial parts of it, so we can develop a sense of lightness. First though, we need to identify the areas that are least effective in helping us move up the spiral. They're the ones that contain the most 'weight.'

Processed foods are readily available but nutritionally and energetically can be devoid of value. They can be quick, fill a gap and be plumped up with fresh vegetables to make them more spiritually attuned to our way of being, but we're still consuming quantities of energetically 'dead' matter. The food is altered from its natural state for the benefit of consumerism and many contain high levels of trans-fats, saturated fats, and large amounts of sodium and sugar. Of course there are examples when this isn't the case, such as milk, which is pasteurised to kill bacteria, or the freezing of vegetables to retain goodness, but on the whole we're swaying towards a society of fast food consumerism where energetic content is rarely considered.

If we want to address this, then we need to incorporate more raw and freshly-cooked meals into our diets. Leaning more to vegetarianism can help, supplementing our diets with seeds, nuts and legumes. So long as our diets are varied, we can provide all the nutrients we need without resorting to eating meat every day. Many believe that we need meat to provide the levels of protein required, however the protein from nuts and seeds not only provides greater nutritive value than that of meat, milk and eggs but it's more effective than these three forms of animal proteins put together.

Try to incorporate at least 20% of organic foods into your diet. The US Environment Protection Agency considers a large proportion of fungicides, herbicides and insecticides are potentially cancer-causing. By reducing the amount of meat we eat, particularly red meats, we're already benefiting from this new way of being. If there's a tendency towards fried foods, opt for a healthier option, concentrating on obtaining the 'good' monosaturated fats instead.

Heavily-processed wheat foodstuffs like bread products clog up digestion. This 'modern' wheat can be quite indigestible due to, for example, wheat glutens causing symptoms of bloating, constipation, fatigue and IBS. Try buckwheat or spelt, or eliminate bread from your diet completely: it doesn't have to be such a staple part of our diet these days as we have so many other options.

Sugars are the bane of our diets; we'll find them in almost everything processed so we need to beware. The 'spikes' in our energy levels are short-lived, since they create a surge in insulin followed by a low, giving a yo-yo effect and making us feel worse than we did before we ate.

Aspartame, the modern day low calorie artificial sweetener, is considered by some as the most toxic additives, containing phenylalanine (50%), aspartic acid (40%) and methanol (10%). When exposed to heat or prolonged storage it is believed that aspartame breaks down into DKP, a toxic metabolite that is not usually found in our diet, the effects of which are unknown. Appearing in over 6000 low or no-cal products, there is concern about it being considered a 'safe' foodstuff. Although much claimed on the internet is anecdotal we must discern fact from fiction. The European Food Safety Authority (EFSA) has brought forward the full re-evaluation previously scheduled to be finalised at the latest by 2020 to 2013.

Under such controversy, is it worth consuming such a product when there are more healthier options?

Steer away from genetically modified foods, there is no scientific research into long-term food intolerance in humans. A genetically modified tomato can have half the nutritional value of an organically grown one.

I'm not a nutritionist but know what works. In fact, we all do, it's just we often don't want to listen to ourselves. There's a huge amount of advice available if you wish to develop a keener understanding of diet in connection to health and spiritual growth. Use your intuition that has been developing, and let it guide you to relevant documents.

When out in a supermarket mentally ask for an image or feeling as you look or hold food. How does it *feel*? What's the subliminal message being fed back to you? It may be lightness or energy, in which case it's right for you, but on the other hand, if it's heavy, low, or slimy, consider putting it back. Some people find that using their bodies as an indicator really helps, holding the food and allowing their bodies to lean in some direction. One way means yes, another no, until over time they've perfected the skill and can almost instantaneously 'read' the energetic content. Try this yourself, hold an organically grown apple in your hands and ask for guidance to see if it is right for you. Which way do you sway? Now take something like offal and see what happens, the difference is amazing. Don't expect this to work instantaneously if you're not used to listening to your intuition in this way, but with practice it will quickly become an invaluable tool to helping you find the right foods to eat.

Walking in nature is fabulous; it freshens and invigorates whilst getting us moving. It also grounds us, attuning us to the earth's energies. None of us can say we don't feel better for just getting outside. Whether we go for a walk or are a bit more adventurous by riding a bike, we'll benefit tremendously. Time spent outdoors is precious and provides us with a sense of calm that's often absent. When we're stressed our cortisol levels go up, resulting in impaired cognitive behaviour, lower immune function and bone density amongst many other effects. We charge around at an extraordinary rate just to maintain a level of commitment to this fast-paced way of life without, often, wondering the reason. By getting outside, away from the noise and pollution of this modern-day world and blending with nature, we're allowing ourselves to take an honest breath.

We can take this one step further by walking in a meditative state. Shut out the world's dramas and all the insignificances that plague us and just *be*. Listen to the birds and the breeze in the trees; notice the little raindrops being held on the leaves, the scent of the flowers and the smell of the earth. See the colours, the extraordinary array of tones and shades, far too many to put into words, and become aware of the peace. Feel the path beneath your feet, the temperature of the air on your face, the insects performing little miracles and *absorb* nature's essence.

Exercise

Start a new resolution to eat more healthily. Empty your cupboards of processed foods and start to plan ways to eat differently. Take it one step at a time, there's no need to make it arduous.

Drink more water, an easy approach that's very beneficial. Buy organic foods when you next go shopping, it may seem more expensive but when we consider how much we waste on a regular basis, if we buy more carefully then we can buy organic foods without it impacting on our budget.

Make time to eat, don't rush, and try to chew your food more. Stop when you're full. Try taking smaller servings to start with until you've gauged what you really need. Never share meals from the same plate! It's a non-starter when trying to eat purposefully, as our inherent need to get enough overshadows the enjoyment.

Involve the family; make it a part of their routine by encouraging them to understand the value of good healthy eating, as well as discovering the joy good food can be.

If you're constantly picking at food, ask yourself why this is. Could it be you're tired, bored or dehydrated? Are you masking an uncomfortable feeling? Look at these options first before diving into the cupboard for a snack. If then you still want to eat, make it something in line with your new resolution.

Go for walks. Get time for yourself away from stress, as well as with family and friends.

Start to research other ways that you can make a difference to your diet - making the effort to discover things for ourselves makes it more likely we'll incorporate it into our day.

Dwell on this

The excellence of nutrition is in the understanding of the energetic vibration it expels.

Section 3

Chapter 12 – Become a visionary

There have always been people who can see into the future. Whether we call them prophets, visionaries or mystics isn't important, it's their skill we're interested in. Some may feel we're insulting these luminous individuals simply by placing ourselves on the same page as them, but in reality we're all just as capable.

In order to understand this ability we need to appreciate the complexities involved. We're not unmasking a mystery to be disrespectful, far from it, we're expanding human awareness for the benefit of all. By finding gems of information hidden amongst the 'clutter' of our minds we're accessing wisdom and our innermost thoughts.

Robert came to see me with much the same problem: he'd lost his way. It wasn't that he didn't enjoy his day-to-day life, because he did, but he couldn't see a future. This is a common enough complaint and one we'll all identify with at some point.

We started by working through the 'frames' of his current life to bring them more into balance, ensuring variety in the process, before realising his problem lay outside of this. His lack of vision and hope intermingled with his lack of self-belief, causing the feelings of having failed. Robert was in his mid-twenties and had no reason to see his life so limited, but without purpose and belief was going to struggle to make the best of it.

Our will to be ourselves is punctuated with other people's opinions of us, exerting undue pressure to 'be successful', when success is a marginal concept in itself. There's absolutely no relevance in comparing skills, and society has a lot to answer for in this respect. Expectations, whether they are of our own making, or society's as a whole, entrench us in a way of being that's not conducive to spiritual growth. We become so tied up with the *need* to accomplish as defined by peers, family pressures, social media and advertising that we forget who we are. We become a clone as opposed to an individual.

If we're emotionally insecure we'll fail to see past these dangers and will quite literally become obsessed with the potential of 'failure.' We'll become ensnared in the negativity and pressure to conform, rather than being individualistic in our approach. We all need to encourage growth and whether we use incentives and directives to help doesn't matter, just so long as we don't take the lead from those who are less 'aware' as a way to feel accepted. This will take us away from our spiritual aspirations and create a sense of unworthiness in the process.

For Robert to have such doubts at his age was heart-breaking, but it highlights society's rapidly degenerative effect, pushing conjecture and spirituality to either ends of the seesaw. If we could encompass our dreams, confidence and self-trust into a medicinal cocktail, we'd feel all the better for it.

Robert started each day with the hope for something inspirational to happen, but it never did. This is because his lack of self-belief confirmed to him that he wasn't worth it, and so he set himself up to 'fail.' To be a mystic in the truest sense we need to entrust ourselves to the highest power, thereby allowing ourselves to 'listen.'

Mindfulness is an important consideration as it reconnects us with source. If we reach a point of self-hindrance but don't get past it, we're not going to make the progress we hope for. This isn't because we don't want to, but because our lack of learning and skills doesn't allow us an entrance. It's much like reaching a gatekeeper at a border crossing and not having the right papers: no amount of driving up and down each little side road is going to change this. It may give the sense of movement, thereby creating the false impression that we're making progress, but if we haven't mastered the lessons on this side of the impasse we're not going to get across.

Overlaying our fears with life-changing decisions may in the interim help us feel less constricted, but if we don't learn the lesson and clear the block, we're not going to achieve our true potential.

Robert's inability to see his future was much like this. He didn't feel he was connected - more that he was sitting on the sideline watching a football match from a distance rather than being a part of it. He needed to get off the seat he'd been sitting on for so long and come down nearer to the checkpoint we just mentioned. If he were to approach this quietly, with a sense of reverence, he'd see that the gatekeeper would be happy to assist. This is like our higher self coming to the rescue. It's not that we're incapable of doing this for ourselves, but there are times when we all need direction (the right kind of course!). Robert's sense of self and confidence were being held back by his need to be sure: he needed to be certain that he wouldn't make any mistakes. He was concerned at being laughed at or thought of as useless. His need to feel secure blotted out his will to find opportunities, leaving him stranded some distance from his wish for inspiration.

In order to do this he needed to create a vision that would strengthen his sense of purpose and make him happy – remember that happiness is an emotional communicator confirming we're on the right track. He needed to mimic the visionaries.

> **"All of us have the capacity to attract to ourselves what seems to be missing in our lives."**
> *Wayne Dyer*

In the old westerns they used scouts to check the lie of the land, and we are going to let our intuition do that for us. We won't get specifics but we'll get a good enough picture to know where we're heading and it will give us a reason to get up!

Take as much time as is needed. We tend to squeeze thinking about important life decisions between rushing about on school runs, watching TV or just before going to sleep, none of which provide the best environment for us to 'hear'.

Eradicate all preconceptions. Often when we've made a decision in the past, it seems to preclude the possibility of changing it. This is habit-forming and shows us as not ready to accept guidance at this level. If this is the case ask yourself why this is. Do you fear foresight and spiritual direction? Are you welcoming 'cloning' to provide comfort rather than being strong enough to recognise opportunity when it's presented?

By behaving as if a past decision has been cast in stone we're limiting our opportunities to grow. We're judging ourselves harshly, after all who hasn't made a wrong decision? But more accurately it's a decision that appeared right at the time but doesn't serve us so well now. That's how we gain our lessons so there's no need for self-judgement, we're all developing and as such alter our perspectives. Just so long as we're honest and upfront with our intentions, we can accept the consequence.

Clarity is an important point; if we're vague we won't get the result we'd really hoped for. Creating a visual imprint will help us and the universe in defining our request.

To become a visionary we need the ability to see the future. We have to allow our true self to speak through us unimpeded, in other words we need to establish a level of connection far greater than a mere conversation, we need to step away from all preconceptions and self-limiting behaviours and free ourselves to work universally.

Robert's lack of confidence and self-belief narrowed his margins to such a degree that he couldn't see a future worth aiming for. Past experiences weren't an issue, as he didn't appear to be staring into his mirrors as a form of distraction: he was quite simply lost.

This is where vision boards or vision books are so marvellous. They allow us a way to reconnect with our true selves without overlaying our thoughts and ideals with guilt or other people's expectations and wants of us. It's a truly invigorating experience. We can be whoever we want just so long as we let go of our focus!

Vision boards aren't just about bringing material things, such as a job, a car or a relationship to us. They can be used more specifically to attract learning experiences to help us move up the spiral.

Manifestation isn't new, but we're becoming more aware of it as the will to succeed makes its demands on people. It's the window to opportunity and abundance that most crave, and it's a wonderful skill to develop. It's quite incredible to think that so many people still resist its charms. They deem it an intrusion into their personality, undermining their abilities to provide for themselves. If you consider for just one moment that manifestation itself is an experience, then we go one step nearer to understanding how unique and powerful human beings really are.

Robert started by going through numerous magazines, using his intuition to guide him. He cut out any pictures that caught his eye and put them to one side. He wasn't concerned with the pictures themselves at this point, just that they attracted him. It could have been the colours, the image or a pleasant memory it triggered. Whatever the reason for including them he didn't let the reason distract him from his main purpose. The more he relaxed the more he felt able to free his mind of all encumbrances. He wasn't using his intuition knowingly, but he'd submitted subliminally, relinquishing any need to control the outcome, and was loving it.

He cut out single words and whole phrases, photographs of people and animals. He didn't confine himself just to material things, but also branched out into metaphysics, astronomy and mathematics. He cut out panels of colours to represent different areas in his life. He didn't narrow his margins by placing any limitations with regards to lack of money or lack of self-belief, he just allowed himself to *explore*.

Once he'd gathered enough cuttings, he sifted back through them to discard any that didn't seem so appealing now, before arranging the remainder on a large sheet of paper. Again he didn't try to work any of this out, he relied totally on his intuition. Once he'd placed them roughly into position, he took a smiley photo of himself and put it in the middle. From this branched out all his potentials.

He stopped at this point to absorb the content of what he was creating. He felt energised, as if a fog that had been encasing him had finally lifted. He could now start to understand his intuition.

There used to be careers offices in every town, where we would go to for careers advice. Now they're mostly situated in schools and colleges, close to the students. Robert had developed his own personal careers office, which he could visit whenever he liked; all he needed now was to learn how to interpret the information.

Intuiting where to place each cutting so as to make best use of his vision board, Robert started to stick the pictures onto the paper where he felt they were most suited. He didn't worry about making it look pretty or uniform, just so long as it *felt* right to him. Sometimes he'd write the odd word instead of using a picture if he didn't have quite the right image to encompass the meaning he wanted. He allowed himself to create in the fullest sense.

Some of what he included was self-explanatory, others less so. This didn't matter, since, if he couldn't intuit the message straight away, he'd leave them for another time when they would have more meaning. He found it enormously helpful to see his life set out in this way, and he felt that he could move forward and start to manufacture the reality.

If at any point Robert felt that a picture no longer held the right energy or what he now wanted for himself, he could either take it off or cover it with something more pertinent. It's not so important to gain an exact replica of the picture, it's the feel we're aiming for. So long as he keeps moving by refreshing his outlook, he'll attain the sense of freedom and fulfilment that he so desires.

In the months that followed, Robert found that not only did he attract much of what was on his vision board, but it freed him from feeling guilty about not achieving. He started to design websites and make video recordings of tutorials. He developed quite a skill in affiliate marketing and, far from considering himself a failure, looked forward to starting work every day.

He looks at his vision board every day to re-energise it, and it looks vastly different now to how it started out. He keeps all the previous ones but every birthday and New Year allocates the day to creating again, encouraging his dreams and aspirations to come even quicker to him.

Exercise

Gather a varied selection of magazines. There's no point having eight on DIY unless that's your sole focus. Define what you're creating. You could be looking for direction, like Robert, or want to energise a specific goal. Decide whether it's a short-term focus, say a year, or longer to give the ethers a chance to provide it within the time spectrum. Try and be realistic with this, don't expect to be a national swimmer by next week if you haven't learnt how to swim yet!

Once you've decided on this, allow yourself to relax, really get into the mood. Turn off the phone and the TV, get yourself some water and, if you wish, put on some soft music. You're creating your future, don't get distracted!

Keep your mind on the task until you feel your intuition has overtaken. Allow it to flow as you are drawn to images, words, adverts or anything else that catches your attention as you go through the magazines. Cut each one out until you feel that you have enough. Sift through them again and discard any that now don't seem right to you.

Get a large piece of paper, or, if you prefer, a notebook. If you decide to use a notebook make sure that you choose one that's a little bit more special than the usual run-of-the-mill kind, so that it conjures up the feeling of being more precious. Don't try to be too organised as you place the pictures, allow your intuition to ramble. You may wish to put a picture of yourself in the centre of the paper or in your book. You can divide either up so that you have sections, each representing a different area of your life such as health, spiritual development, family, work, relationships, exercise etc. It's your life you're creating, so you decide what you want it to contain.

Have fun with this, there's no point in getting overly serious. The more you relax and enjoy yourself the more your intuition can guide you.

*Once you're happy with the general layout, you can start to manifest your dreams. Stick your pictures in with loving intent. Energise this every day by reconnecting with the energy that you had when you created it. **Believe** you have the life you would wish already.*

Some people may wish to use this as a self-development tool. If so, ensure that you've defined this before you start otherwise you may not get what you want! Allow yourself to be drawn to pictures and words that create the feeling of who you want to be. Gather a collection that has meaning to you in some way; maybe they bring back memories, or remind you of people you admire. It can help if you allow words to jump out at you, to turn your attention to certain areas that may need work, such as forgiveness, trust or love.

Be compassionate and non-judgemental. We're creators in the truest sense of the word and as such are hugely powerful. We can be whoever we want, just so long as we believe it.

Dwell on this

The times are changing and yet we're impervious to wisdom

In Conclusion

We've been creating a solid foundation to develop from, but it's by no means complete. What we've learnt through this book isn't necessarily going to sort out all of our problems but it'll go some way in helping us to make sense of them.

The more we develop, the greater our understanding and appreciation of how the world works. It's not always going to be that we can alter a 'for instance' or adapt a 'maybe' but we can certainly give it a go. How we attract and interact with people on a personal level will become more significant as we develop a better understanding of ourselves.

But let's not forget who set us up for this development in the first place. We're surely not thinking we came across this book by chance! We're all part of a huge network where universal connection provides an enormous amount of wealth in terms of wisdom and advice. If we're prepared to accept this then maybe we're prepared to go that step further and look at the spiritually acceptable form of chance where sign-chronicity isn't just a play on words but a way to get a message across.

If we allow ourselves to accept that all that happens does so for good reason, then we're going to be that much nearer the truth where purpose and responsibility are combined into a sim-plex (a simple but complex) analogy of self.

Synchronicity isn't about observing life's coincidences as if an anomaly; it's a life form in itself raising questions about the world the live in, who we are and the purpose of being. If we allow wisdom to come through in this way we're encouraging spirituality in a form that's both enticing and significant. What we want is to be part of a spiritually-attuned environment where grace and love are at the heart of everything we do. In order for this to be the case we need to *take notice*: ask questions of ourselves, be 'connected,' don't allow lower vibrational interference and most of all be honest. When we've absorbed and understood these influences we'll feel a huge shift towards spirituality.

What we have and how we behave isn't just what we're concerned with as love and grace form part of a much worthier concept. Whether we call this God, Buddha, Allah or any other honourable title isn't of relevance, it's the universally enigmatic power of self that's so important.

By observing the words and phrases that 'come to mind' and how we 'play' with our vocabulary, often without realising it, ensures our spiritual direction. If humour appears it's even more likely to come from higher levels intent on trying to get a word in!

Appreciate the wisdom in the so-called 'old wives tales,' there's often more to them than we realise, e.g., the colours and imagery they have introduced into our terminology. 'Seeing Red' is often expressed when we're angry or have 'lost' our temper, but have we considered where this expression comes from? The red energy associated with our base or root chakra gets expelled at force when we're in this state, causing it to shoot straight to our heads allowing angry thoughts and words to 'escape' us. The base chakra is the first of 7 main chakras depicting our etheric self through energy centres placed the length of our body and head. Its primary function is to allow a sense of self, connecting with earth energies and related functioning of organs in the pelvic area.

If we're impressed with wealth we should ask, 'What is so attractive?' Everything has a greater value than the cost on the price tag, we just choose to forget this. Are we stuck in a consumerist society where wealth in terms of the money in our bank accounts and the possessions we have hold more importance than love and compassion? There's nothing wrong with wealth per se, we'd all like to feel free of debt and the worry that surrounds it, but if we're swaying towards consumerism, and neglecting our inherent wish to help other people by following the consumer road, then we're becoming unbalanced. Greed and materialism make us unhappy, there's no doubting this, but we're often hoodwinked into thinking we *need* things purely because we lack confidence in our own abilities to be the best judge. We've been led rather than been asked to follow, a subtle but important difference.

Advertising is largely responsible for this as it bombards us with images of health, happiness and success even though we're not going to achieve it purely by buying the product. Of course we all know this, but it can leave us with a sense of not being good enough or failure even, drawing us into the illusion without realising we have the choice.

Rather than covet bigger or brighter things or more up-to date models, let's bring our sense of fairness and free will into line by reconciling desire and comfort. As we do, our need for possessions will diminish easing the pressure on our incomes.

This is all part of the circle where life repeats. As much as we're aware of the cost of an item in terms of pounds and pence, do we consider its value in the hours spent at work to earn it in the first place? I don't suggest we become overly obsessed with this as it can lead to repetitive cycles, but to appreciate its true worth in terms of the energy we give gains us an insight into understanding wealth from a higher viewpoint.

Money is simply energy in a solid form. If used wisely it gains us a level of expression that far exceeds mere frittering. If we're not respectful about this our level of self-worth is reduced, propelling us into a more consumer-led society where compassion and love become less valued.

"What is a cynic? A man who knows the price of everything and the value of nothing."
Oscar Wilde

I'm not advocating 'tightness' (as this pushes us to the other end of the seesaw) but respect for everyone who contributes to the economy, no matter the format. State benefits, gifts and inheritances are but a few ways in which we receive, often without appreciating what it's taken to accumulate that 'wealth' in the first place.

If we consider the purpose of our characteristics, we could describe them as karma's influence. Some may think this a bit strange as karma is more often associated with correcting a past wrong, whether in this life or a previous one. But what better way to achieve this than through our character traits? What we're blessed with as we come into the world is a mixture of 'vices' which we can then work out through our lifetime, relinquishing the 'debt.' These can easily be distinguished through the akashic records imprinting on our karmic voice at the time of birth - in other words, our astrological charts. I'm not trying to convince anybody of this, just introducing the concept for further discussion. You may choose to email me your thoughts.

The world as we know it lacks soul at times but we can all make a huge difference. Whether we take this in the literal sense by addressing our daily commitments is up to us, but the spiritual purpose is somewhat different. If we each do our part by raising our vibrations by moving up the spiral towards the pinnacle of success, we're starting to create a far kinder world to live in. We'll draw in and encompass a whole new way of being purely by becoming spiritually attuned. We're connected through a universal language where colour, race or creed isn't of relevance, we're all just one of the many that recognise the importance of love and how it heals.

If one of us commits by attuning to the higher vibrational energy that we've talked of so often in this book it will make a difference. Multiply that countless thousands of times and we'll reach a point where cause and reaction alters the polarity and hence creates a positive shift, making the world a better place to live!

If we're concerned about this it can cause a block. Let's each take responsibility for our own journey and see how the effect ripples out. We may even wish to take this a step further by committing to a life of service, devoting ourselves for the sake of the planet. Please don't take this in the sense of dogma or subservience, it's nothing of the sort. It's a glorious way of being where wisdom and grace benefits us all, encouraging progress and self-love in the process.

Work through this book several times and each time you do you'll adapt further. You'll notice change within yourself, within your families and friends until ultimately you'll make a universal difference.

And that's what this book is all about, not to develop purely for mankind's benefit, although who would complain if we did, but to develop transitionally. We're bettering ourselves as we work out our less-developed traits and characteristics bringing compassion, understanding and forgiveness closer to our hearts, whilst all the while imprinting positively on those we come in contact with. If we struggle to overcome a given character trait let us not denigrate its appearance in someone else. Let's see it as a lesson for ourselves to work with and be grateful for the help.

We all want to make the best of ourselves but often the lessons can be challenging, bringing pain and hardship to the fore. I admire everyone who rises to this as the more difficult the journey, the greater the level of purity that can be achieved. We're all part of a community where we're lovingly cherished and are never alone.

Step back from self-pity and petty-mindedness and become more individualistic. Live purposefully where thoughts, words and deeds reflect *our* soul's choice, not others willing us to copy them. Should we forget this then we should bring back our sense of compassion and kindness without chastising ourselves, no matter how often it happens. We're not perfect so let's not make perfectionism a rod for our own backs.

Attraction is a force to be reckoned with and its power should never be undervalued. Whether this is attraction to an object, person or situation is somewhat academic, as it's the attitude to the outcome that's important. Be open and approachable, but not overly malleable as people will take advantage. Look at what a person attracts in terms of their nature and fate; what is it about their associations and ideals that draw you and are you going to benefit from such an attraction?

For my part I commit to expanding human consciousness. Whether we live alone or with our families, learning to balance our traits is a good place to start. We're here for a reason and if ours is different to someone else's, let's acknowledge this and give them the freedom they need to accomplish it. If we each show a little humility it'll go a long way in helping us achieve our goal - that and conscientiousness. Pay attention to the little things and don't be flamboyant. Often it's in the small that we can make the most effective difference to the big – the dynamism between microcosm and macrocosm. Free yourself from prejudice and 'agendas,' allow others to live as you would, encouraging positive influence and growth.

In the coming months and years we'll see a swing towards spirituality where generosity of spirit and encumbrances are poles apart. Developing attitudes of self in line with good morals will enhance our self-respect, encouraging good behaviours and considerateness.

Bless each of you for reading this book and, should you wish further information or indeed just wish to get in touch, please do so via my website.

www.maryancillette.com

Traits Tree

Below are a selection of traits that can be monitored by use of a traits tree. Or make your own, listing characteristics that seem more pertinent. Watch as they come towards the middle the more you work on them. Truly Life Changing!

Me

Responsible	——————————	——————	Irresponsible
Lazy	————————	————	Hard working
Good	———————	——————	Bad
Honest	——————	———————	Dishonest
Caring	——————	————————	Inconsiderate
Selfish	——————	—————	Thoughtful
Loyal	———————	————	Disrespectful
Generous	——————	—————	Mean
Controlling	——————	—————	Charitable
Romantic	——————	—————	Platonic

Idealist		Realist
Attentive		Neglectful
Victim		Bully
Exciting		Boring
Immature		Mature
Responsible		Irresponsible
Taker		Giver
Open		Closed
Arrogance		Humility
Addictive		Disassociated
Adventurous		Staid
Confident		Insecure
Energetic		Sluggish
Critical		Encouraging
Jealous		Trusting
Happy		Sad

Notes

Notes

Notes

Notes

About The Author

....

Mary Ancillette was raised on a smallholding in the Surrey Hills, where caring for the animals was her only true passion.

Since then her love of people has grown through the knowledge of her soul purpose, revealed to her in a dream. She has focused her efforts on developing spiritually to be able to help others.

Trained in various therapies, Mary encompasses much of what she has learnt both through traditional schooling methods and self-development to arrive at the place she occupies today. Preparing to use her experiences to help guide others, she has started to develop a brand name – Life-Changing Moment – as a way to bring awareness of the benefits of self-development to the world as a whole.

As a therapist Mary works concurrently on the physical, mental, emotional and spiritual levels to bring peace of mind and healing to all those brave enough to confront their fears, recognising the need for self-improvement. Whether highlighted through illness, lack of purpose or some other cause, Mary ensures their relief, encouraging self-belief by an honest approach.

If you wish to contact Mary you can do so through her website www.maryancillette.com

She would be very pleased to hear from you.

Perfect Choice

Mary Ancillette

This book is a perfect choice for those who want more from their days.

On one level it's a simple love story. On a whole other level, its clarion call for all of us going about our days wishing for a better life but who never take Right Action to make things happen.

Was Jeff reckless or brave when he spoke to Diana on that life-changing commute?

Is Diana right or wrong to suppress her innate talent for tuning into messages from above?

For all of us, the signs are around and the clues present themselves to us daily.

Fortune favours the brave and fools should always rush in.

This debut novel from the pen of Mary Ancillette is a reminder to us all that there is no such thing as a Perfect Choice. Not making any decision at all, though, is simply not an option.

It is a reminder too that souls sometimes have to lose themselves, and each other, in order to find their way back home.

Completely Novel

ISBN number 9781849144223